The Good News About Careers

The Good News
About
Careers

HOW YOU'LL BE
WORKING
IN THE
NEXT DECADE

BARBARA MOSES, Ph.D.

Best-selling author of *Career Intelligence*

Jossey-Bass Publishers • San Francisco

Copyright © 1999 by Barbara Moses.

FIRST JOSSEY-BASS EDITION PUBLISHED IN 2000.
THIS BOOK WAS ORIGINALLY PUBLISHED BY STODDART PUBLISHING CO. LIMITED,
34 LESMILL ROAD, TORONTO, CANADA M3B 2T6.

Jossey-Bass books and products are available through most bookstores. To contact Jossey-Bass directly, call (888) 378-2537, fax to (800) 605-2665, or visit our website at www.josseybass.com.

Substantial discounts on bulk quantities of Jossey-Bass books are available to corporations, professional associations, and other organizations. For details and discount information, contact the special sales department at Jossey-Bass Inc., Publishers.

 Manufactured in the United States of America on Lyons Falls Turin Book. This paper is acid-free and 100 percent totally chlorine-free.

Library of Congress Cataloging-in-Publication Data

Moses, Barbara.
  The good news about careers : how you'll be working in the next decade / Barbara Moses.
    p. cm.
  Originally published: Toronto : Stoddart, 1999.
  ISBN 0-7879-5269-9 (alk. paper)
  1. Career Development. I. Title.

HF5549.5.C35 M67 2000
331–dc21   99-049949

FIRST EDITION
HB Printing
10 9 8 7 6 5 4 3 2

*To my son Nathaniel
and to the next generation:
may you live and work well.*

Contents

Foreword

*T*his is a book about the world of work. We complain about work, often experience stress as a result of it, but it is a critical part of our lives. Work is, of course, about economic survival, but more importantly it is at the heart of our humanity. It helps define our identity and sense of self, our ability to contribute to an organization, community, society, and our families, and to grow and develop as individuals.

This is the world that Barbara Moses knows and writes about so well. I met Barbara in the early 1980s. We have had countless conversations about work and careers over the years, some funny, some serious, some absurd, some creative and thought-provoking. In my view, Barbara is at her best as an observer and commentator on the world of work.

This book provides practical strategies and techniques that can be used by everyone to increase their marketability and personal satisfaction in the workplace of today. Barbara gets behind the buzzwords and describes how you can be more effective in communicating in a frenetic world, how to make the most of your opportunities to network, how to prepare yourself for an increasingly uncertain future, how to career-proof your children, how to be a better coach to others — as well as how to be more "coachable" — and how to choose work that you will enjoy and at which you are most likely to be successful.

All of these tactics and techniques make for extremely insightful and useful reading, but I believe the real value of this book is even deeper. I read the manuscript in two long sessions while I was on holidays. As I finished it, I was struck by the unique perspective that characterized the writing throughout. What came across was enlightening, compassionate, and humorous at times, but more than that it actually caused me to *think*. The areas being discussed are an everyday part of my life as a human-resources consultant working with large corporations. Many concepts have become the equivalent of unassailable truths — networking is always good, busy is better, you need to be an extrovert to be successful, and everyone who is highly evolved as a person loves getting feedback.

As I read a different and original point of view on each of these topics, I was forced to question some long-held ideas. Then I thought about how seldom I do *that* anymore. I realized that one of the true losses in our frantic and time-impoverished lives is an understanding of the value of reflection. We are so obsessed with doing, with being productive all the time, that we no longer see the benefits of taking time to think differently about ourselves, our situations, and the way things are. And isn't that ability what separates us from the animals? As Socrates said, the unexamined life is not worth living.

Finally, despite painting a realistic and accurate picture of the challenges facing us in today's world of work, Barbara ultimately presents us with hope. The good news is that there really is greater flexibility and room for variety in how we work. There are people loving the new world of work and thriving in a host of different circumstances. If you believe there is room for greater meaning in what *you* do for a living, then I recommend that you read on. Take the opportunity to reflect, make some choices for *you*, and reposition your own views on work and its importance in the total fabric of your life.

JANE HUTCHESON
Senior Consultant
Hay Management Consultants

Acknowledgments

I'm privileged to count as my clients, colleagues, and friends some very insightful and committed people. This book is full of their stories. I have worked with many people in many organizations and have learned from all. Unfortunately, space does not permit me to thank each one.

I would like to thank the following friends, clients, and colleagues for their anecdotes and wry insights: Helen Bozinovski at Heart and Stroke Foundation; John Bryan of Core International; Heather Campbell at Nesbitt Burns; Carolyn Clark at CP Hotels and Resorts; Sue Cunningham and Debbie Glover at Lattice Learning; Heather Faire at PPG Industries; Michelle Gerber at PricewaterhouseCoopers; Margo Gordon at Warner Lambert; Keith Hollihan at Linkage Incorporated; Susannah Kelly at Herman Smith Executive Initiatives; Pam MacIntyre at Crown Life; Margot McKinnon at Body Harmonics; Jeff Novak; Anne Peel at Voices for Children; Lauri Reed at CTG; Harvey Schachter; Connie Simington at Enbridge Consumers Gas; Keith Southey at CIBC; Barbara Steinberg at the United Nations; Irene Taylor; Nadia Valerio at Bank of Montreal; Judy Westover; Leslee Wilson; John Young at Four Seasons Hotels and Resorts.

Acknowledgments

I have been fortunate to gain insight into young professionals as a result of the leading-edge work of the public-accounting firms. I thank in particular the partners and education leaders I have worked with, including Wayne McFarlane, Chris Gillespie, and Judy Elliott at PricewaterhouseCoopers; Lori Pearson and Halia Bonner at Ernst & Young; Michelle Johnston at Deloitte & Touche.

My many clients should be congratulated on the outstanding work they have done in helping people respond to new work realities, in particular: George Sallay and Darlene Brushett at the Bank of Montreal; Sharon Wingfelder and other leaders in the Royal Bank Learning Network; and Sharon Rose at the Nortel/CAW Return to Learning Program.

I owe a special debt of gratitude to my long-time colleagues and friends Tamara Weir-Bryan and Joan Hill, whose insightful observations, generosity, and outstanding work have nourished me, and to my other committed associates: Laurie Hillis and Ann Toombs in Calgary, JoAnne Maurer in Vancouver, Frank Rambeau in Ottawa, Denise Lapointe in Montreal, my American associates Joan Caruso and B.J. Chakiris, Elaine Christie in New Zealand, and Howard Elias in Hong Kong.

Thank you Bill Pallett at Delta Hotels and Resorts for your outstanding generosity and friendship; Garth Toombs of Garth Toombs & Associates in Alberta, and Dick Knowdell of Career Research and Testing in California, for your consistent and long-time support. Also, my fine speaker's agents including Speakers' Spotlight, CanSpeak, and National Speakers' Bureau, and the associations and organizations they represent, for linking me up with audiences who are a constant source of inspiration and real experiences.

Thank you also to my friend and literary agent Bruce Westwood and Gordon Pitts, my wonderful editor at the *Globe and Mail*, who has given me free rein in my column writing. I remain grateful to the team at Stoddart and in particular thank Don Bastian, my fine editor; wry marketing whiz Stephen Quick; and Mary Giuliano, my savvy publicist.

Acknowledgments

Thank you Jane Hutcheson and Jeff Davidson for your thought-provoking, sometimes irritating, and always stimulating conversations.

This book could not have been written without the extraordinary support of my husband, Andrew Weiner, the toughest and most insightful editor, and the best partner, anyone could ask for.

Introduction

When my book *Career Intelligence* first came out, two years ago, people recognized it as an accurate description of the new workplace. But many found the description — of a world without any certainty or job security, where every individual must take responsibility for managing their own career, and where one must constantly reprove one's competence — scary and depressing.

Since then, however, I've noticed a shift in how people feel about the changing landscape of work. While they recognize there are tough realities associated with the new employment contract and the new work order — including the constant uncertainty and the sheer volume and pace of work — many have also found in it significant reasons for celebration.

Rather than simply saying, "Well, this is the way it is, there is nothing I can do about it," people are starting to take what I've called an activist stance in relation to their careers. They are engaged in active thinking and dialogue about how they work, why they work, and what they need to do to earn a living.

As I show in this book, individuals are finding creative and fresh ways to manage some of the complexities of a life on fast forward. They are more open, not only to change and to experiencing the exciting aspects of a new career but also to sharing their feelings and experiences. They are looking for work that reflects who they are, for work in which they are free to bring their entire personality and spirit.

If there is any phrase that captures the new thinking about work, it's *take it personally*. Work is no longer experienced as an impersonal force of nature over which one has no control. Instead people are asking, indeed demanding, that work meet their personal needs. Everywhere, people are questioning what I call in this book the "cult of busyness" – the preoccupation with doing, acting, and achieving for its own sake, rather than being mindful of what we care about and what we are trying to accomplish.

At the same time, organizations are also beginning to recognize the new personal realities of their employees' over-committed, hyper-metabolic lives and to make some accommodations. In this book, besides helping individuals create a better work future, I will examine ways of shaping more *life-friendly organizations* that are in tune with individual rhythms and the human need for challenge and emotional security.

It's not all good news out there, of course. A friend of mine, a vice-president of a large financial institution, was asked whether she wanted to see a scary movie. She said, "I have a policy against seeing scary movies these days. If I want to be frightened, I just go into work in the morning."

Organizations continue to slash overhead costs and associated payroll and to obsessively monitor the bottom line; parents continue to be spooked about the prospect of their kids not making it in the new workplace; organizations continue to be puzzled about how best to manage under the new deal at work; boomer bosses are perplexed by their 20-something staff (not to mention children), who seem to have a very different attitude towards work; and everyone is grappling with the competing demands of managing very complicated work and personal lives.

In this book, I don't pull any punches. I describe some of the more hard-hitting truths, the scary stuff, if you will, about work and how we'll be working over the next 10 years. But at the same time, I see much to be optimistic about.

Over the course of the past two years I have been encouraged by the number of people who have found interesting and inventive ways to craft a future that allows them to withstand whatever curves the economy might throw at them. Many people have also told me that as little as three years ago they couldn't have possibly imagined themselves having made such a successful adaptation to an uncertain work world – much less finding real joy and liberation in new ways of working.

Freedom, flexibility, opportunities to test yourself in new roles . . . these will be the cornerstones of life and work in the next decade. As traditional authoritarian workplace structures crumble under the onslaught of the new economy, people are gaining a new sense of *control* and *autonomy* in their lives and careers. A new style of worker is emerging, based on a new, unique psychology.

What are the new workers like? What motivates them, and how does that differ from what motivated their predecessors? What will they need to do to be successful? How will organizations need to rethink how they reward, motivate, and retain people? These are some of the questions I address in this book. I also look at:

- where careers are going, and how we, as individuals, managers, and parents, can profit from future work trends;
- how to operate as a self-managing career activist;
- how to achieve a creative balance between the new work and personal realities;
- the search for authenticity in a shifting career landscape; and
- how managers and organizations can lead today's and tomorrow's workers.

Introduction

There are numerous myths about the new workplace, such as: in the future you will constantly need to reinvent yourself; in order to market yourself successfully you will have to become a walking billboard of your accomplishments, endlessly networking and parading your skills; in order for your children to be successful they should be crammed with as much extracurricular skill-building activity as possible, while being encouraged to make early career choices.

In this book I challenge conventional wisdom and show you how elastic the new workplace really is. There are many ways to design work that plays to your own strengths, preferences, and values. I show how to use this elasticity to your benefit — and that of your children.

One of the questions I ask early career professionals in my workshops is: "Do you feel that your parents and managers understand the impact of the new work order on your future career?" Sadly, only a handful of people indicate that their parents or managers do understand.

In this book, I present and answer the questions I am most asked by 20-somethings about how to kick start their careers. I also share what boomer bosses think of their young workers — and vice versa — and how managers can engage their young staffs.

How can parents career-proof their children for this new work world? This continues to one of the most pressing challenges facing us as parents and as a society. Indeed, of all the issues I write and speak on, this is one of the ones that elicits the most intense response. As you will see throughout this book, I believe that we can create a work world that we would be proud to pass on to our children.

And that will be the best news of all.

The New Workplace

The Cult
of Busyness

*L*inda, a senior vice-president in the financial-services industry, just got back to the office from a vacation at the cottage — a week early. "I was calling in every day on my cellphone, checking e-mail on my laptop, faxing memos back and forth . . . and still I had to be there. My kids are mad at me, my husband is mad at me, but what can you do? The work has to be done."

Jim, a former geologist, has been semi-retired for years, although hardly anyone knows it. Jim has deeply internalized society's belief that visible work equals visible worth. He takes frequent vacations, but tells his friends and neighbors that he is going away to look after overseas business interests.

Both Linda and Jim are, each in their own way, victims of what I call the cult of busyness. Today, one's busyness is worn like a badge of honor, a measure of one's status in the modern workplace. Ask someone how they are, and almost invariably they'll say something like, "I'm so busy" or "Things are crazy around here."

It's become almost banal to comment on how busy and overworked people are today. While the unemployed and underemployed complain about not having enough meaningful or challenging work, people with full-time jobs have too much. Statisticians document it, journalists report on it, almost everyone complains about it.

"I Work, Therefore I Am"

To some degree, of course, this frantic pace of work is driven by economic realities. Organizations demand improved productivity and competitiveness to please demanding shareholders and other stakeholders. Employees, uncertain about their job security, scramble to comply.

But there are other factors at work here. Somewhere along the way, many people have become addicted to this relentless, hyper-metabolic pace of work. It's almost as if they need to be continually *doing*, *acting*, and *achieving* to feel fully alive: "I work, therefore I am." Even when they seem to be complaining about the pressure they are under, they are actually making a kind of *boast*: "I'm so busy, therefore I must be important." It's as if you need to be demonstrably over-committed and exhausted to be a fully functioning contributor to your organization and paid-up member of the global economy.

Indeed, it's interesting to see what happens to these people when, for whatever reason, they are forced to stop in their tracks. One comment you often hear from people who are between jobs or work assignments is the feeling that their life is empty. As one person put it, "I'm starting to feel like I'm a phantom, that I'm not real. There's nothing that gives my life shape or meaning."

Other people are profoundly ambivalent about the new work realities. If you ask them in workshops how they are feeling, they will tell you that their most significant relationships are suffering. When asked how they would like to spend their time outside work, they say, "Forget spending time with friends, just spending time with my children is a luxury." They are tired, distracted, grumpy. But they don't see any way out. "I have no choice," they say. Typically, in fact, it is those who complain the least about their busyness, the quietly desperate ones, who are suffering the most.

Consider Carol, a 45-year-old single mother with two teenage children who works as a human resources consultant. "Lately, every time I schedule a family event or outing such as a birthday dinner, I have to cancel at the last minute because of a so-called important meeting," she says. "At this point, my children don't believe me when I make a commitment to them to do something with them. It's just the way it is." Despite the fact that her children are experiencing difficulties at school, she couldn't make the last parent-teachers night. She used to work out, but she hasn't done anything for the past year. Every time she thinks about her life she gets more depressed, but feels that she's caught between meeting her financial commitments and her children's needs.

But whether people embrace busyness or resent it, they rarely stop to question it. If you ask people *why* they are working so hard, you find that most people haven't given any thought to it: It's simply the way things are. Busyness has become a fact of nature, like the weather, or gravity.

The Price We Pay

Ultimately, though, we may pay a heavy price for our unthinking acceptance of this ever-escalating cyclone of busyness. You have to wonder: What will be the long-term impact on people's physical and mental health and on their personal relationships? And what, exactly, are we teaching our children about work?

A few years ago, when I gave a talk about careers to my son's Grade 6 class, I asked the students what they thought their parents felt about their work. The children started to compete about whose parents were more miserable: "My mother hates her job." "Oh yeah? Well both my mother and father hate their jobs." "At least your parents have a job to hate." And so on.

Children develop many of their initial ideas about work from what their parents say and from what they observe for themselves. Is it any wonder that they develop the belief that work is unpleasant? This impression is exacerbated by their resentment for the tremendous number of hours their parents work, and the intrusion of work into their family's time together. Many feel abandoned by their parents, who seem to prefer to meet their never-ending work commitments. An educational psychologist colleague tells me that a significant number of the children she sees suffering from behavioral and cognitive difficulties say, "I'm so lonely."

Similarly, I often hear the 20-something children of workaholic baby boomer parents express resentment about their abandonment in favor of work, along with cynicism about the ultimate payoff of those sacrifices. "My father worked for the same company for 25 years," one young accountant told me. "He worked nights, weekends, vacation days. We never got to spend any time with him. He worked his heart out for them. And when he was 50 they tossed him out like a piece of garbage. I'm never going to make the mistake of believing that my work is more important than my personal life."

Boomer managers sometimes complain about the attitudes of their 20-something staff, their reluctance to put in long hours, and their emphasis on balancing work and personal life. I find it a healthy development, and one that may well be a more adaptive response to the future of work.

Work in the future will almost certainly be of a more *intermittent* nature than it is today. Rather than working continuously for the same employer for a long period of time, more and more of us will move between assignments or contracts of varying lengths with different employers or clients, punctuated by varying periods of so-called downtime. During these periods we may be looking for work, or upgrading our skills, or simply re-energizing ourselves through personal pursuits.

We will need to be able to manage these periods of downtime not only financially but *psychologically*. We will need to know not only how to be busy but how to *stop* our busyness, how to use these breaks as times to nourish ourselves, reconnect with people, explore new avenues of work and play. We will need to find something other than our own busyness to validate our self-worth.

What Organizations Can Do

Although we may not have the power to change the way that people's sense of self-esteem has become attached to being productive, we can lobby inside our organizations. What behaviors are valued?

For example, are meetings routinely called at 7:00 in the morning or at 6:00 at night or on weekends? Are vacations interrupted at the behest of anxious customers? Is it okay to take off in the middle of the day to help out at your kid's school? Do you have to cancel training events at the last minute because managers say they're too busy?

One of the key steps in creating what I call "life-friendly organizations" is to provide people with the opportunity to reflect on how they are living their lives and spending their time through career planning or self-assessment. Here people have the opportunity to reflect on such questions as:

- Is your work really meeting your most important needs?
- Are you defining yourself purely in terms of your accomplishments?
- Why are you working so hard? To what personal ends?
- Are you making significant sacrifices in favor of your work? What is the impact of your work on other people important in your life?

One executive vice-president in the financial-services industry invited his department to a career-management experience with the following words:

"You've given us a significant investment of your time. Now it's time to invest in yourself. Take this day to think about your work and your life and how you can be as satisfied and meaningfully engaged as possible."

The New
Obsession with Work

*R*ecently, at the hairdresser, I overheard a 20-something reception-ist telling a teenage assistant: "Don't quit school. Did you know that a university education today is worth what a high-school education was worth 10 years ago?"

Everywhere, people today are talking about work: How to find it, how to keep it, how to get greater satisfaction from it, how to control it so that you still have a life. This new obsession with work, and the sophistication with which people are talking about work, is symptomatic of a profound sea change in our society.

When I went to university in the late 1960s, like so many of my generation I didn't particularly consider whether my education would be instrumental in finding work. To the extent we thought about work at all, we assumed opportunities would be available. Indeed, there was a definite snob-bery among liberal-arts students about our more "careerist" contemporaries who were pursuing professional degrees with clear-cut job prospects, whether engineering or accounting or physiotherapy.

Of course, people *have* to be highly career conscious today, with the stakes being so much higher than they used to be. Work, particularly "good" work – challenging and with decent pay and professional content – has become a highly valued commodity. And the specter of ending up as one of the have-nots instead of the haves creates ever-intensifying anxiety in a society that is increasingly divided.

What are the consequences of this new work obsession? On the one hand, people who don't have work – from newly graduated 20-somethings to so-called early retirees – are desperate to find it. But among people who do have work, there is a growing tendency to reevaluate how they are spending their lives. They are asking: "Why am I working so hard for so little – financially, emotionally, and personally? What is the cost of this work to my family, to my relationships, to things that are important to me?"

This is not the same thing as a mid-life crisis. It stems from a realistic reappraisal of the relationship between effort at work and traditional rewards such as advancement, salary, status, and protection against the vagaries of the marketplace. As these extrinsic rewards diminish, people pay more attention to the *intrinsic* qualities of their work, asking: Is it skill-building? Fun? Challenging? Does it provide opportunities to balance work and personal life? While these qualities were always important, they have become much more salient today as work is stripped of its traditional rewards.

Essentially people are saying, "I may no longer be able to aspire to the traditional trappings of success. But that gives me the freedom to make life choices that reflect my needs and values." Obviously these choices will be moderated by economic realities. But increasingly, people seem more willing to make tradeoffs, giving up more work and income for more time for family and personal interests.

Ultimately, this reevaluation of work and its rewards may prove liberating for individuals, freeing people to make decisions independent of traditional pressures and to pursue personal passions rather than the brass ring.

At the same time, this new hyperconsciousness about work may be a healthy trend for society. As more people actively *think* about how and why they are working, it is to be hoped that this will lead to a dialogue about the nature of the contemporary workplace, the distribution of work, and the new employment contract between individuals and organizations.

Living and
Working in TempWorld

Ken and Doug, camera operators with a network news organization, worked side-by-side for more than 10 years on similar assignments. They now find themselves victims of downsizing. The two men are equally employable in terms of their portfolio of skills and experiences. But where Ken has lined up various freelance assignments, Doug sits at home, depressed and immobilized by his unemployment.

The major difference between them is that Ken, who had been working on a renewable temporary contract, has always seen himself as a freelancer, even though he was with the same employer so long. All along, he has maintained an active network and sought out information about the assignments of his counterparts working for other employers. Doug, in contrast, was a permanent, full-time employee and continues to see himself as someone who needs a conventional job.

In many ways, being a temporary worker is more a state of mind rather than a hard-and-fast employment status. And in this sense, it often seems to me that the world is divided into two types of people.

Some people like to think of themselves as living in a world that is unpredictable and ever-changing. If they have a job, they view it as one step in a series of short-term commitments to a job or organization. That commitment may stretch out several years, but they still have the mindset of temporary workers. For them, too much predictability is boring and stifling.

But there are others who, no matter how much turbulence they may have experienced in the employment market, still believe in the fundamental rightness and goodness of the traditional employment contract. Often, they have been the victim of downsizing or reengineering in a number of job settings. And yet they still crave the "security" of a conventional full-time job and react with anxiety to a lack of predictable employment.

This latter group is still very much in the majority. A recent poll, conducted for Shell by Peter D. Hart Research Associates and reported in the *Globe and Mail*, found that 72% of the 1,123 randomly selected adults who participated in the survey said they preferred "the security of staying with one employer for a long time and moving up the ladder."

Unfortunately for this latter group, the conventional, full-time, "permanent" job is a rapidly vanishing commodity. Today, like it or not, we all have to see ourselves as temporary workers, no matter what our official employment status is. We may have something that *appears* to be a conventional full-time job, governed by a so-called traditional employment contract. Or we may, like a steadily growing proportion of the workforce, be contingent, contract, or freelance workers. But either way, we are living and working in what I call "TempWorld."

Everything Is Temporary

In TempWorld everything shifts rapidly. Nothing is forever, everything is temporary: where you work, what you do there, the skills you use, the people you work with. Or, as the late Andy Warhol might have put it, in the future, everyone will have a good job — for fifteen minutes.

In TempWorld, as in Hollywood, the past counts for little or nothing. You are only as good as your last hit – or presentation, or quarterly results, or sales figures. Whatever your experience or accomplishments, you have to constantly re-earn your right to employment. Under such circumstances, work becomes an endless audition as you constantly re-prove that you have the savvy, skills, and know-how to be the "best person for the job."

As one person put it, "Just when you think you can relax for a minute, despite the fact you've been killing yourself and achieved outstanding results, there's another reorganization and there you are, résumé in hand, reciting your list of accomplishments over the past six months."

I like to compare the new career pattern to a date, the old one to marriage. Many of us crave the relative security, comfort, commitment, and intimacy provided by marriage. But marriage can also be, well, predictable. A date, on the other hand, can be exciting. You don't know how it will end until you get there. But you always have to hold your stomach in.

Young Workers Show the Way

For many people, the new work realities demand a very difficult adjustment. Organizations used to offer more than just job security. They also offered people a sense of *psychological* security as well – a feeling of belonging to and contributing to something bigger than themselves. Now, in most organizations, that sense of psychological security is gone, leaving people feeling unprotected and without moorings.

There are considerable generational differences in how people respond to this uncertain new work world. Many pre-boomers and baby boomers mourn the loss of stable and predictable employment. Under the old psychological contract between the individuals and the organization they had felt protected, experiencing both financial and career benefits from that protection.

In contrast, their 20-something and early 30-something counterparts never learned to expect a secure and stable work environment, and so have a completely different set of beliefs about work life. Unlike their pre-boomer and boomer predecessors, they often welcome the challenges of this new and unpredictable work world.

For the past seven years, I have been working with early career professionals in public accounting firms. A few years ago, when asked about their future aspirations, a significant percentage saw partnership as a viable and desirable career goal. Although some see partnership as a possible career goal, they can also think of any number of other options: moving into industry, owning their own business, working for themselves, perhaps even running a café.

Of course, even within the pre-boomer and baby boomer contingents, there have long been those who, whether by accident or design, have embraced temporariness: freelancers, consultants, contract workers, and the like. And when we compare these people with those who have pursued the security of full-time employment, we see that in most respects – in education, experiences, skills – they are similar if not identical. The primary difference is *attitudinal*.

As one 40-something woman, a highly successful contract worker, put it, "I love going from contract to contract, even if at times it's a bit scary. Each assignment is different, so it's an opportunity to learn something new. And then, I get bored after a while, so I like knowing there is a discrete end and I can move on to something else."

Her words reflect a key underlying psychological dimension. For some people the very idea of a predictable work relationship is stultifying. They thrive on change, on testing themselves in new situations where the outcome is uncertain. Indeed, when provided with too much security they become depressed and look for ways to undermine their security by making career-endangering moves. When they find themselves in relatively secure environments they say things like, "I feel like I'm being choked."

Where some people embrace temporariness, others have it forced on them. Can these reluctant temporary workers, with no previous predilection for risk and change, make the necessary attitudinal shift when they find themselves thrust into an insecure work world? In many cases they can.

Jack, a longtime editor, was forced into freelancing by the closing of his magazine. Initially, he saw this as a way of "keeping his show on the road" while he looked for another "real" job. But real jobs proved elusive – while freelancing proved to be highly rewarding, both financially and personally. "The more feedback I got on what I was doing, the more confident I was in my ability to do it well," Jack says. "I realized that I could make it on my own, and I found that very liberating. All those years, I wanted to belong to something. Now I belong to myself." Two years later, when he was offered a plum full-time editing job, Jack turned it down flat.

Ultimately, there is little difference between freelancing and a supposed full-time job. Today, we are all free agents. Like multimillionaire sports stars, we go wherever the work takes us, changing jobs or assignments with the ebb and flow of the economy, seeking to better ourselves in terms of challenge and rewards. And like sports stars, too, if our services are no longer necessary, or considered too expensive, we will be cast aside. The key difference is that the freelancer – the psychological free agent – already has the mind-set to move on quickly to the next challenge.

Tips for Living and Thriving in TempWorld

Think like a temporary worker: Even if you have a so-called "permanent" job, start to think of yourself as a temporary worker. Temps know they can make no assumptions about any kind of predictability in their work.

Temporary workers know that it is up to them to demonstrate that they have the skills for the job – now. They will not receive any kind of training to bring them up to speed, so it is up to them to get whatever training they need.

In TempWorld there is no tolerance for error, no protection for a job less well done. Social Darwinism is at work, and competition for resources is fierce.

Earlier, I compared the old career pattern to a marriage, the new one to a date. Let's extend that comparison to temporary work. In a marriage, both sides will often be prepared to slog it out when things are not moving along in the happiest manner. But in a date, there is no serious commitment on either side, and when the going gets tough there are no serious consequences – emotionally or financially – to ending the relationship.

Under these circumstances, all relationships need to be redefined. For example, workers should look on their bosses as their clients. What are their critical business priorities? How is your work contributing to their goals and adding value to the enterprise? Are you managing your relationship with your boss with the same care and vigilance that you manage your relationship with clients and customers?

Try to define yourself in terms that are independent of your job title. For example, would you describe yourself as a comptroller for ABC Trust Company, or do you consider yourself as a financial professional, with business-planning and problem-solving skills, adept at working with diverse teams, currently applying your knowledge in the financial-services industry? Think of yourself as having a portfolio of skills that you could potentially apply in a variety of work settings.

Build financial independence: Temps know they cannot afford to make any assumptions about economic continuity. If you lost your income tomorrow, do you have sufficient savings to tide you over until you find a replacement source of income? Financial planners typically recommend that you keep six months' salary in the bank to provide you with the barest level of protection.

Ensure your marketability: Although you can't have job security, you can have security in the *marketability* of your skills. If you had to find new work tomorrow, do you know what skills you could sell? Do you know who to contact as potential buyers of those skills? Are your skills sufficiently broad that they have a number of possible business applications? Or are your skills tied to only one industry or one narrow business challenge?

Going through a process of self-assessment will help you know your product: the skills you have to offer, the kinds of environments in which you are most effective, and the ways in which you can add value to an employer or client. At the same time, you can enhance your self-confidence by evaluating your past accomplishments, in both your work and personal life, and the skills you used to achieve them.

Keep your portfolio up to date: With constantly changing work and shifting skill requirements, "lifelong learning" has become a necessity. Moreover, in our hit-the-ground-running business culture, it's up to you to do what is necessary to ensure the currency of your skills portfolio. Stay current in your field and continue to develop skills and knowledge outside it.

TempWorld offers many challenges to how we think about working life, as well as opportunities. Or as Frank Sinatra sang in "That's Life," you may be shot down in May, but you're "back on top in June."

Life in TempWorld
1. You will always have to re-prove yourself.
2. Success is conditional on your last hit.
3. You are affected by external factors and may move up and down economically, subject to these factors.

4. Your skills portfolio, interpersonal skills, and resilience will help safeguard you against external factors.
5. Relationships will be fluid, and you will have changing alliances as you move in and out of different projects, assignments, work situations.
6. There will be more commuter families as individuals go "where the work is," leaving others behind.
7. Communities will weaken as people leave family and friends to chase work opportunities globally.

If you want to thrive in TempWorld you will need to take personal responsibility for your career and your life. Understand future work trends so that you can be best positioned to seek out and make the most of every opportunity.

On Being
a Player

Dave, 50 years old, recently "early retired" from a large accounting firm. After spending close to a year on a job search, he came up with two offers: one, a well-paying position with a company in a suburb, the other part-time, and for less money, but in the financial district of a big city. He took the big-city offer. "Getting up in the morning, putting on a suit, and walking around all those tall buildings makes me feel like I'm still part of the action," he said.

Thirty-three-year-old Carol is torn. She wants to take 10 months off to "paint, think about things, test myself in new ways, feel what it's like to not be working." She can afford to do this, but feels held back by one concern. "What am I going to tell people if I bump into them on the street? It's not like I can say I'm taking time off to spend time with my children, or to go back to school. People will think I don't count anymore, that I've lost my edge."

Fifty-five-year-old Peter has just sold his very successful business in a deal that leaves him free of any financial concern for the future. And yet he is desperately pursuing new business ideas, however unsuitable. By Peter's own admission, these ventures are more appropriate to someone half his age. Nor do they make good use of his skills as a highly accomplished professional who still has something to contribute.

What do these three people have in common? They all want to be players, they all want to be "in the game." Our society uses work as its currency to determine an individual's worth. So much of our sense of self is tied up with working, doing, achieving, and, most importantly, being *seen* to be achieving. And for some people, being a player is so crucial a part of their self-image that they make unusual or even misguided career choices to keep that status.

Being seen to be a player means you are important, an opinion-maker, a mover and shaker, someone who is going somewhere. Players are engaged and connected. Other people seek out their friendship and support. To not be a player is to be unimportant, almost irrelevant, inconsequential.

Sarah, newly downsized and disengaged from the workforce, tells a story of bumping into a former supplier at a party who used to actively cultivate a relationship with her. "When I told him I was no longer working, I saw a flicker of what looked like pity in his eyes. Then he just got up and walked away, as if I had ceased to exist."

This is truly a tragic reflection on what we value today. Most of us complain about the demands of our work, yet it does provide us with a vital source of identity and self-esteem. Many people say that if they could, they would stop working. But most of them, if actually confronted with that as an option, would likely continue working anyway. And successful small-business owners often refuse to let go long after they should, because their whole sense of identity is tied up with their business.

By the same token, we feel uncomfortable around people who aren't working. We have trouble finding a point to connect with, and we even feel sorry for them, as if they are no longer valuable contributors to society.

Players and Non-Players

Who wants to be a player? Obviously, everyone wants to feel important, to feel they are doing work that makes a difference. If the opposite of being a player is being a schlep, no one would tell you that they want to be a schlep. But certainly, some people are more driven to be players than others.

Everyone has different views on what it means to be a player. For some it means being in the know, having your hand on the pulse, being connected. For others, it means being a leader in your field, or being an innovator. And for yet others it means being the best. Many talented professionals and accomplished artists have left their field once they learned that they would fall short of greatness: being "really good" was just not good enough.

For some people, *where* they are a player is as important as what work they are doing. Linda, for example, a human-resources consultant in a large financial-services company, was offered the opportunity to be the vice-president of a high profile organization in the public sector. But she worried that being in the public sector wasn't as sexy or high profile as being in financial services. I've come across this quandary many times: people are attracted to working in the public sector but worried they will no longer be seen as a player because the work is not as closely related to the bottom line.

People are motivated to become players for different, although sometimes overlapping, reasons. One common element is the search for some kind of *recognition* or acclaim – being seen as making the best deals, getting the biggest advances, or having the largest consulting firm. But people differ in the *kind* of recognition they seek.

For some, the only acclaim that counts is the *public* variety, as measured in newspaper inches and TV appearances. But for others the playing field may not be so public. Some "players" turn to a relatively small community for their acclaim. For example, the back-room boys quietly wielding power behind the scenes, or the key adviser to the CEO. They are in the thick of things, with the people and in the places where big decisions are made. It doesn't matter to them whether the public knows about their contribution, as long as they are recognized as players by their peers.

This hunger for recognition, whether public or private, may or may not be tied to a drive to achieve. Some people are happy just to be *seen* as players: to have the title, the corner office, the high profile. But for others the title is not enough. You actually have to *own* the achievement, to have done something only *you* could have done. Typically, for this group, the achievement must be *quantifiable* – whether it's the size of the deal, the return to shareholders, or the number of employees working for you.

Some people cannot bear to be "one of" – that is, one of 20 computer programmers or one of 10 human-resource consultants. Jenny, for instance, took a cut in pay to be *the* director of marketing for a small organization, rather than one of any army of analysts working for a large organization.

There are also people who have been thrown into the game reluctantly. Because they have to work, they feel *forced* to become a player, and at this point their competitiveness kicks in and they find themselves playing hard. But at best they are ambivalent and uneasy. All things being equal, they would rather not be in the game.

For many, the desire to be a player likely can be traced back to childhood, as reflected in some children's excessive achievement strivings to be the best at whatever they do, or in children who constantly put themselves forward to be in the limelight whether to star in the school play or play the class clown.

Witness Pulitzer-prize-winning columnist and best-selling novelist Anna Quindlen. She told Jan Wong in a *Globe and Mail* column of how her "perfection complex" at age 16 drove her to "get all A's, be editor of the school paper, be a cheerleader. I wanted to be a star."

High expectations, though, are not always met. When we are young, we are seen as having all kinds of potential. But by the time we are in our 40s, we have largely played out that potential. By then it's apparent whether we are players or not. Many people in their 40s are grappling with the recognition that they will never be the players they thought they would be. Facing up to that reality can be a very painful adjustment, indeed.

The Dark Side of Being (or Not Being) a Player

Unfortunately, there is almost always a point when you "lose it" and fall out of the game. Perhaps the market takes a dive, business has turned sour, or someone younger and more capable has arrived on the scene. For those so heavily invested psychologically in being players, the price is huge, as their very sense of self is challenged. As television personality Ralph Benmergui told the *Toronto Star* of his own highly checkered career, "I think there's a certain lack of puffiness in what I do because I had to deflate myself and no longer be a major motion picture inside my own head." Players unable to adjust to life in the minor leagues may retreat and fall into depression.

Typically, players are never satisfied. They become addicted to the adrenaline rush of being "Mr. or Ms. *It.*" Witness, for example, the number of highly paid CEOs who complain that they must retire at the age of 67. They are driven by a hunger that can never be filled. Instead of taking joy in achievements and tasks, they look for the next set of challenges to be overcome, the next mountain to be scaled.

Others seem unencumbered by the need to be a player. They can make life and career choices free of the burden of image. Being in the limelight, being seen to be doing work of visible prestige and status, simply are not important sources of their self-esteem. They are not motivated by external validation, or by the need to wield power and influence. Unfortunately, there is a downside here as well. Because they care little for prestige or status, they fail to seek out high-profile assignments perceived to have importance to management. As a result, they may be regarded by managers and colleagues as apathetic or uncommitted to their work. And yet they will often complain about being passed over for work that they would enjoy doing.

We are all motivated by different things. The key to going after what you want and making effective career decisions is being aware of what makes you feel important. Know yourself. If you want to be a player, don't be embarrassed about it. Some people, especially women, feel it's somehow unseemly to want to be a player, or to demonstrate the necessary competitiveness to become one.

Try to identify what it means to you to be a player, and identify the stage on which you wish to play. Instead of simply driving to become a player in your professional life, look for ways to be a player in your whole life.

What We
Didn't Do on Vacation

*T*here is a new epidemic in today's workplace . . . weariness. Recently, I put a question to a workshop for some 200 middle managers and first-line supervisors in customer-service work. I asked the attendees to identify their personal goals. What came through was a palpable feeling of being depleted, of having nothing more left to give. Almost to a person, they said their goals were to be reinvigorated, re-energized, renewed.

Most of these people, I thought, could benefit from a good long vacation. But I knew that they were unlikely to get one.

Taking a vacation used to be a simple matter. You booked your time off, and away you went. But in today's time-urgent, compressed workplace, what was once a simple decision has become fraught with complexities.

Harry, a sales manager, was finally able to get away with his family for a one-week vacation. But he was called back after five days to soothe an important customer.

Linda, a communications specialist, studied her vacation options for months, finally settling on a kayaking vacation in the Yukon. "I work so hard, and my free time is so precious, that when I do get away, I want to make sure it's a really meaningful experience."

Mel, a senior manager, recently returned from two weeks at the family cottage. "It was great to be reading and canoeing and fishing," he says. "But coming back to work was a nightmare. There were the usual thousands of faxes, e-mails, and voice messages, but I just couldn't motivate myself to process it. Re-entry was a real problem."

Laptops at the Beach

How do you stack up? Do you take your full allotment of vacation days? Do you completely de-wire while on vacation, or do you routinely check on e-mail and voice-mail? Are you able to mentally disengage yourself from work or is your mind back at the office? Do you return from vacation refreshed and reinvigorated? Do you come back feeling you have had a great time but looking forward to getting back to work?

Leisure experts suggest that most people need two consecutive weeks to really benefit from a vacation. But for many people today, that is no longer a viable option. The pressure of work demands and deadlines is such that they are able to get away for a few days or at most a week at a time. Even then, like Harry, they may be called back early to deal with some real or imagined crisis.

How often, these days, do you get someone's voice-mail only to hear, "I'm away on vacation this week but I will be calling in to check my messages." How often do you see travelers toting their laptops along with their golf bags, so that they can continue to work on that proposal or gather up their e-mail, or carrying their beepers and cell phones to the beach? Under pressure from both employers and customers, people feel unable to make a clean break — and technology makes it that much harder to do so. The result: vacations don't accomplish what they should.

Organizational expectations can weigh heavy. As one professional reports, "In my organization, long days are demanded, vacation weeks are often postponed, and all-nighters are all too common. These expectations are underscored by a second in command who works late – sometimes until midnight – most nights, works almost every weekend, and whose one-week vacation turns into three days off because she finds it necessary to be in the office. The company has a policy of allowing all employees to take four Fridays off in July and August. In reality, many of these are not taken, either because workload won't permit it or because senior management schedules important meetings with you and clients on the very days you have booked off."

Those who do swim against the current and take exceptionally long vacations often create consternation among their colleagues. "I wish I could afford to get away for so long," they say, meaning, "*My* work is far too important to let me get away for so long."

Then, too, many people seem afraid to take a longer vacation for fear of what will happen on their return. They know that, like Mel, they will face a mountain of work that has accumulated in their absence, but with a diminished will to get through it. "Every time I start to really relax, I pay the price," Mel says. "I start to question why I'm working so hard all the time. I lose my edge. Eventually I get back up to speed. But it's always a struggle."

Indeed, some people worry about whether they'll be able to rev themselves up sufficiently after vacation to go back to what they've been doing. It's almost as if they feel their commitment to work is so fragile and tenuous that once out of the work environment they will lose it completely.

The decision of how much vacation time to take becomes a kind of cost-benefit analysis: "How relaxed can I afford to get? Do I take the kind of vacation I need and suffer the consequences later, or do I take a shorter vacation and minimize the downside when I get back to work?"

And then there are those who fear that if they go away for an extended period of time, their employers will discover that they can manage well enough without them. We might call this the Ted Baxter syndrome, after the classic episode of the old *Mary Tyler Moore Show* in which newscaster Ted is forced to take a vacation, and discovers that he is all too replaceable. After a decade of downsizing, this may appear a perfectly reasonable fear.

The self-employed may find it even more of a challenge to take a vacation. They worry about losing customers, missing potential sales – the out-of-sight, out-of-mind anxiety. Then there is the question of whether there is anyone they can trust to cover for them while they are away. Along with these complexities, they may also have difficulty in disengaging, because so much of themselves is tied up with what they do. Many small-business owners are so overly identified psychologically with their business that when they are away from it for any length of time they lose their sense of meaning and direction.

The self-employed can also be victims of their own empowerment. Because they are in charge of what they do and when they do it, they can in theory take a vacation any time they choose. On the other hand, there is no compelling reason to take a vacation at any given time, or indeed to take one at all. There is no one telling them when to take off, and they are not going to lose any paid vacation days.

Productivity Suffers

In the short term, organizations may appear to benefit from having employees so willing to cut back on their vacation time. But there is a longer-term cost. Ultimately, exhausted and depleted staff are not high-performing staff. Indeed, intelligent organizations might well wonder about the *emotional wellness* of individuals who do not insist on taking the time they are entitled to in order to refresh themselves.

To their credit, at least some organizations have become concerned about people who never take a long enough break to be properly refreshed and rejuvenated and have taken steps to discourage such compulsive "presenteeism." They have tried to communicate to their staff the importance of taking a vacation by limiting the number of vacation days staff can carry over from one year to the next. Some innovative organizations have gone even further, treating additional vacation days as a negotiable benefit staff can "buy" – reinforcing the value of vacation time in people's minds. Similarly, some organizations encourage staff to take sabbaticals of up to six months to engage themselves in new pursuits, whether it be trekking in the Himalayas, landscape gardening, or volunteer work. Organizations who have adopted these strategies report that they are reaping gains in creativity and productivity.

Such enlightened attitudes, however, remain the exception rather than the rule. Most organizations continue to tolerate, even encourage, their people's avoidance of longer breaks, while many managers think nothing of interfering with their workers' vacation plans.

Consuming Leisure

As average vacation times shrink, many people are gripped by much the same imperative that drives their work: to do more with less. It's no longer enough just to have a pleasant break. Instead, people feel driven to cram a month's worth of experience into a few days. Whether it's helicopter skiing or white-water rafting or climbing Mount Everest, it's almost as if we've become so tired and jaded that an ordinary vacation doesn't do it for us anymore – we need a Technicolor experience to experience it at all.

Then, too, we have become so accustomed to acting, doing, and achieving that we become uncomfortable when confronted with the blank canvas of leisure time. So we buy an experience to fill it.

There's an element of conspicuous consumption here as well. That African safari may be enjoyable in itself (or it may be dull and grueling), but the experience of it is immeasurably enhanced by being able to brag about it when you get back to the office.

Even when people go away to a retreat, there is often the same tendency to reduce experience to a consumable commodity. Indeed, when presented with a menu of stress reducers, people may get even more stressed out deciding what to do. "Should I go for homeopathic medicine at 10:00 or aromatherapy? Should I do Pilates or go for a 10-mile hike?"

For the most part, then, what we *don't* do on vacation is what we could benefit from most: relax and recuperate from the strains of work, and renew ourselves through personally meaningful pursuits.

Why the Grass
Isn't Always Greener . . .

When I was young, I would look into the homes of my Christian friends and neighbors and wonder at the delights and treats and family bonhomie that lay beneath the twinkling lights. It was only when I was an adult that I realized how romanticized my beliefs were. Christmas, although joyous for many, can also be fraught with disappointments, repressed tensions, and bubbling resentments.

There are certain times of the year, such as post-vacation September and just after New Year's, when people return to work with feelings of disappointment, looking at their day-to-day lives with a jaundiced eye. They believe secretly − or not so secretly − that other people have better jobs, make more money for less work, get better bonuses, are more appreciated by bosses and colleagues, have work that better meets their personal needs, and just generally have more fun. They believe, in other words, that the grass is greener elsewhere.

This myth of the better job − or life − next door, or perhaps across the street, is widely held. Partly it stems from the tremendous pressures that people are under today. People everywhere feel overworked and under-rewarded. It's not surprising that they tend to overestimate how much fun other people are having at work, while underestimating their own career and life satisfaction.

This belief is also formed, in part, by a lack of understanding of workplace realities. I do a lot of work with early career individuals in professional-service environments. Their picture of the working world is largely excerpt-ed from stories told by their friends. So, for example, they will insist that professionals in private sector companies make more money than they do and are paid double time for any hours over 35 in a week. When challenged about the origin of their beliefs, they almost always mention the proverbial friend's friend.

For many people, the notion that the grass is greener elsewhere is exacer-bated by the notion that it was somehow an accident that they have ended up in a particular professional course – that they never really *chose* to become what they've become. Looking back, it all seems arbitrary, somehow: If a particular company had not been aggressively recruiting on campus, or if a friend had not referred them to their employer, or if they had not made a spur-of-the-moment reply to a recruitment ad, they would not have embarked on the series of events that culminated in their doing the work they are doing now.

If your career choice was an accident rather than a matter of choice, if it seems to you that you merely "fell into" what you are doing, you might well ask, "How do I know I wouldn't be happier doing something else?" This is, in fact, the most common type of career angst one sees among educated managers and professionals in First World countries.

When people believe that the grass is greener elsewhere, the danger is that they will jump jobs or careers prematurely. Instead of doing a thorough assessment of both their short-term interests and long-term needs, they move on at the first opportunity, in the belief that all kinds of things will work out in their new job. Unfortunately, in many cases, they discover that their new job is not a panacea — that in many ways they were actually happier before. Moving on may solve one problem (for example, getting a higher salary) while creating new ones (bad management, tighter resources, etc.).

Rather than jumping from an imagined frying pan into a real fire, you should first take stock of your current situation, and ask: In what way is it meeting my needs, both in the short- and long-term? What am I giving up by staying where I am? What is disturbing me? How will moving on lead to my achieving greater fulfillment?

Interestingly, when people go through a meaningful and rigorous self-assessment, they typically discover a number of things. First, they learn that they have indeed made career choices. Rather than being the servant of a series of accidents and arbitrary career events, they have gravitated into certain areas because they were good at them and because doing that type of work was satisfying. By the same token, they have moved away from work situations and environments that did not play to their personal preferences and aptitudes.

They also often discover that they are enjoying their work much more than they realized. It's just that one or two things have taken on disproportionate significance in coloring how they feel about their work. For example, 33-year-old Jane, after a self-assessment of what she really cared about and what she was good at, observed, "Hey, I really like doing what I'm doing. The only thing that's really bugging me is that I'm not getting enough recognition and I guess now that I've identified that I can do something about it."

Similarly, people often will say, "Although there are one or two things that are disturbing me — and I'm going to look for ways to minimize them — on balance, when I look at all the things that are positive, these things seem to pale in importance."

Living in Real Time
Effective career management means making informed choices. You may not

be able to get everything you want right now, but you may be able to get much of it. For example, in the short-term you may choose to put up with a boss you don't particularly care for because you are being exposed to a new technology and are getting great experience.

As a general rule, however, the older you are, the less flexible you should be about making tradeoffs. I thought it odd when a highly accomplished 45-year-old engineer was going to move into what he described as a "killer environment" where he would be working 80 hours a week because the experience would look good on his résumé. At what point, I wondered, would he see himself as living in real time, as opposed to continuously upgrading his credentials in preparation for some imagined future where he would at last be rewarded for his sacrifices.

Sometimes, of course, it is time to move on – not necessarily because your job is horrible, or because the grass is greener elsewhere, but because it is too easy to be lulled by the daily predictable comforts of a well-worn routine. Perhaps it's time to test yourself, to go out on the edge, put yourself on the line.

The path to renewal may be across the street, or it may be in your own backyard.

part two

The New Worker

The Search
for Authenticity

*I*n my 20s, while completing my Ph.D., I worked under contract for a large petrochemical organization. Coming from a family of small-business owners, I thought corporate life the absolute height of glamour.

Desperately hoping this contract position would lead to full-time employment, I studied the behaviors, dress, and deportment of the successful women in that organization and tried to emulate them. But despite my best efforts to "act corporate," I did not receive a job offer. I was torn between extreme disappointment and relief. In retrospect I realize that the awkwardness of my impersonation, and the ambivalence behind it, must have come through.

Sacrificing the Self

Traditionally, much as in the book *The Man in the Gray Flannel Suit*, "acting corporate" has meant being "in role," wearing a mask, donning a false persona, numbing yourself: never letting people know what you're really thinking, never displaying too much enthusiasm (you might say "that's quite good" but not "that's wonderful!"), never being emotional or self-expressive or spontaneous.

But where once people accepted the need to conform to corporate norms as a fact of life, today there is a widespread perception of organizations as demanding the sacrifice of individual selfhood.

Across the board, from senior managers to the most junior employees, people are no longer so willing to act different from "who they really are," repressing important aspects of their personality, in exchange for employment. More and more, people list the need for personal authenticity among their key criteria for satisfying work. It's not only "I want challenge" or "I want a good salary" but also "I want to be myself at work . . . I don't want to have to hang up my values and personal style at the door."

Women, of course, have always struggled with the demand to check their emotions and expressiveness. For example, Sandra P., a senior manager in the communications industry who has an amazingly loyal and committed staff, has often been criticized by her executives for being "too complimentary" to her staff. They say she is too effusive, too open. Basically she is too Technicolor for them, too willing to show her hand. "What kind of world are we living in, when you're criticized for being enthusiastic?" she asks.

Similarly, it was no accident in the 1970s and 1980s that many women railed against a "dress for success" dress code based on the thoughtless and silly feminization of the male suit, designed to make them look as sexless as possible.

Although women may have borne more of the brunt of having to fit into what many of them experienced as a hostile culture based on traditional male values of toughness and competition, this is certainly not an exclusively female issue. When David P. was fired from his senior-management job in manufacturing, his life went into a tailspin. As he went through a rigorous self-assessment as part of his outplacement, he realized that he had spent the last 15 years "first play-acting, and then *becoming* that role. I had become someone I didn't like — cold, impersonal, obsessed with the bottom line — and in the process had sacrificed some of my most fundamental values. And I had bought into a lifestyle to support my role as a senior executive that had nothing to do with what I cared about as a person. I lived where I was supposed to live, sent my kids to the right private schools, played golf even though I found it pointless and boring."

Generational Pressures

When I asked a group of 20-something engineers working for a civil engineering consulting firm what was most important to them in a job, one man said, "Being able to be my authentic self at work." His comment was met with widespread agreement.

The search for authenticity has become a major issue for 20-somethings, who ask questions like:

- "What's the big deal about a second hole in my ear as long as I'm well-groomed?"
- "Why can't I wear jeans to work if I'm not meeting with a client?"
- "Why can't I work closely with important customers without being micromanaged?"
- "Why can't I take time off to run in a marathon if I'm putting in the hours to make up for it?"
- "Why do I have to give up my personal life to get ahead?"

This is a generation that grew up in a period of social, economic, and environmental upheaval, when all traditional North American values were being questioned and all our institutions were under fire. It is not surprising that they are so irreverent and detached, so lacking in respect for traditional organizational norms. It's not like the "suits" have done such a great job, they say.

Indeed, if the organizational climate is now shifting to allow people greater freedom of dress and expression, it is at least partly in response to pressure from these authenticity-seeking 20-somethings. Organizations are increasingly aware that if they want to attract, hire, and retain the best of this generation, they need to accommodate their demands for a freer environment.

Of course, the nature of the people who run organizations has changed, too. The pre-baby boomer generation who once dominated organizational life are heading into retirement, taking with them a set of values shaped by Depression and war that stressed the need for hard work, sacrifice, and toughness.

Taking their place in the upper reaches of the corporate hierarchy are front-end baby boomers, born in the late 1940s and 1950s. These boomer bosses are more sceptical about the value of corporate conformity, and more tolerant of diversity. They are also, in many cases, themselves working much too hard in their downsized organizations to sweat, in the way their predecessors might have done, the small details of what's acceptable versus unacceptable behavior.

When Work and Personal Boundaries Blur

Alongside this demographic changing of the guard, the structure of organizations has been changing, too. The old hierarchies are breaking down under the pressure of new technology, a newly diverse workforce, and new ways of working such as project work and, in particular, telecommuting.

It's not surprising that research shows that telecommuters are happier than other employees. For one thing, telecommuting provides enhanced flexibility in the use of time — allowing individuals to better balance work and personal life. But perhaps just as important, it permits something closer to a seamless connection between work domains and personal domains. For example, if you want to work in your pajamas while listening to Bach, or have your lunch at 3:00 in the afternoon, you can. The more time people spend outside traditional work settings, the freer they feel to be who they are – and the greater the "slippage" from organizational norms. One of the more common comments I hear from telecommuters is that when they do have to go to the office, they forget what is considered acceptable dress.

Marsha G., a long-term bank employee who now telecommutes, describes the blurring of boundaries this way: "When you do come into work, you bring more of your personality with you. Every time I come in, people say, 'You look so happy. You can't be working hard enough – you don't look very stressed.'"

The example set by these telecommuters helps to subvert the norms even for those who remain in the office as they gradually start to set new standards for such things as dress, office hours, and behavior.

The sheer pace and pressure of contemporary work life is also helping to raise consciousness of the cost of inauthenticity. It's one thing to have to conform a little when you're working in a job you enjoy in a relatively convivial environment with time to reflect and prospects for promotion. But when you're working 80 hours a week under intense pressure to produce in exchange for what you see as insufficient rewards, that's a long time to spend being something other than yourself. People start to ask themselves: *Why* am I doing this? Is my work really meeting my needs? What am I giving up?

The recent upsurges of interest in spirituality in the workplace, as demonstrated by the number of conferences devoted to this topic across North America, is testimony in part to this hunger for authenticity at work. So is the increasingly influential movement towards "voluntary simplicity," in which people give up their high-paying jobs and luxurious lifestyles in favor of doing work that reflects their real needs and values.

It could be argued that this new hunger for authenticity is fundamentally a First World luxury, a privilege of highly educated people who have a range of choices. And indeed, when your primary concern is simply to put food on the table, you can't afford to spend much time worrying about whether you are acting in tune with your authentic self.

But when you do have choices, you should exercise them. Ask yourself, "What is the cost to me over time of working in a job that's not a good match for me?" For short periods, we may indeed be capable of making tradeoffs, doing work that represents less than a good fit with our interests and values in favor of pursuing other goals. But in the long term, we pay a heavy price when we deny our need to live an authentic life.

What Kind of
New Worker Are You?

*T*he project team had gone the limit, putting in several all-nighters and weekends to meet a demanding deadline. Management, in turn, put a lot of thought into choosing their way of expressing appreciation: an alarm clock with a big gold company logo, and a hundred-dollar-a-plate dinner at one of the city's fanciest hotels. They were therefore puzzled by the response of team members. Instead of responding with gratitude, most of the people looked, well, disappointed. "It's enough that I gave them my soul for the past four weeks, I don't want to have to go to bed and wake up with them," commented one of the team members, 27 years old. Another person enjoyed the dinner and the company of his co-workers, but said, "My idea of fun is not putting on a suit and eating in the kind of restaurants my parents go to."

Across the street, a similar organization called together their staff to celebrate the outstanding quarterly results they had just posted. The CEO said, "I wanted to thank you for your superhuman efforts. I'm not going to take up much of your time. I just wanted you to know that you are each going to get a cheque equal to five per cent of your salary. And you can choose an additional reward from a menu that includes extra vacation time, club memberships, or course or conference tuition." People walked out with huge smiles on their faces.

These examples illustrate some of the ways in which rewards can go awry from intention to reception – and some of the ways in which rewards can delight individuals when they are customized to individual needs and preferences.

I am often asked, "How do you motivate the new worker?" But there is really no such thing as a single type of clearly definable new worker. Today's workers do have certain shared experiences, attitudes, and beliefs, including an awareness that in an uncertain work world it is up to them to plan and manage their careers and keep their skills portfolio updated. But they also bring to the table a complex constellation of psychological motivators.

People are different, in other words – and this is hardly news. Still, the range of motivators driving today's new workers is broader than ever. And people have become much more assertive in expressing their individual preferences.

Understanding your own motivational profile can help you identify what is most important to you in a work setting. For managers and organizations, understanding the profile of staff members can help in designing effective rewards and systems to attract and retain the best talent.

I have grouped what motivates the new worker into six idealized profiles. While each profile has its own defining characteristics, individuals may share characteristics from more than one:

Independent thinkers or entrepreneurs: "I need to be free to choose and be in charge of what I do, for whom, and when." These independent problem-solvers want to own or build their own work, whether working inside an organization on a project or in their own independent business. They are impatient with corporate norms and procedures and have little allegiance to the corporation. Hanging around the office too long or being forced to go to an endless round of meetings makes them antsy. They are motivated by autonomy, and need to feel they are living in a free-form world that they can shape.

Almost by definition, independent thinkers are uncomfortable with "received wisdom," preferring to create or invent their own way. They are prepared to take full responsibility for their successes and failures. But in order to do so, they have to be in charge. They also need to be doing work that in their own terms is meaningful and has impact — whether it is a project important to management, the development of a new customer-retention strategy, or the creation of their own business.

As employees, independent thinkers are responsive to having money at risk — whether a bonus, commission, or other type of pay for performance. Hell for them is the off-site "team-building event" complete with highly pro-grammed activities for golf, tennis, and the scavenger hunt that allow them no freedom of choice.

Lifestylers: "I work to live, not live to work. I want to enjoy my work, but it's also a means to an end. I want the flexibility to pursue my own personal passions." A range of people fall into this category: young resort workers who want the opportunity to pursue their love of outdoor activities; 30-something parents determined to balance their work and family life; mid-career individuals saddled with eldercare responsibilities along with commitments to children; young professionals who value the freedom to pursue personal priorities.

As one example, many young professionals I work with in Vancouver say they would be loath to take a transfer to a bigger job in Toronto, because it would take them away from the mountains and into harsh winters. They are typically prepared to work hard to do whatever is necessary to get the job done. But they expect their hard work to pay off, by buying them free time they can enjoy in the way they prefer.

Personal developers: "As long as I'm learning, I'm happy." This category includes many 20-something contract workers, frequent job changers, as well as independent consultants. Most Information Technology professionals fall into this group.

Personal developers evaluate their work in terms of whether they're being stretched, or whether they are acquiring a new skill. They are very quick to become bored, particularly if they are in what they see as a dead-end job. Although not risk-takers by nature, they are prepared to take career risks if it will stretch them or expose them to a new arena in which they can acquire new skills.

Personal developers are not without ambition. For many of them, it's important to advance in their careers and become players in their profession. But their identification is very much to their profession and their work, and not to any particular employer.

Interestingly enough, despite most people's beliefs about young MBAs being motivated primarily by money, nearly half of 1998's crop of U.S. business-school grads turned down their highest-paying job offer, opting instead for ones that offered more room for personal growth (*Business Week*, May 22, 1998).

Careerists: "I want to get ahead, and I am willing to make the necessary sacrifices." Obviously, this category is not new. In fact, most careerists resemble the profile of traditional baby boomers who evaluated their success in terms of opportunities for advancement and increasing work responsibility.

Although some careerists want to be players in their profession, they are more likely to want to move into general management. They tend to take a longer-term view of their career, but differ from the old-style careerist who saw a predictable future within a given organization. Although they are prepared to entertain the possibility of having a long career with their present employer, they also recognize it could just as likely take place elsewhere, and their horizons are more likely to stretch across an entire industry, several industries, or types of work settings.

Careerists are ambitious, motivated by prestige and status. They recognize that as they move up the ladder, they may be moving into other areas that reflect increasing responsibilities. A young lawyer looking down the road, for example, may equally see himself as partner in a large firm, a chief corporate secretary, or head of his own firm.

Authenticity-seekers: "I gotta be me." Individuals motivated by authenticity refuse to "hang up their personality" at the door. They won't sacrifice their own personal expressiveness in order to play a corporate role. Don't ask them to put on a uniform, or to repress their personal values in favor of "what's good for the company."

In some ways, this group shares characteristics with the independent thinkers, because of their demands to be self-expressive. If they run their own business, they will typically infuse it with a strong personality that reflects their own style.

Authenticity-seekers can be quite creative, but difficult to manage if their employer demands conformity to corporate norms. This does not mean they cannot be happy working for an organization under any circumstances. Indeed, many disaffected mid-career changers complaining about the soullessness of the corporate sector's pursuit of the bottom line have moved into the not-for-profit sector to do work more in line with their personal values.

Self-expressive 20-somethings choosing to work for a small, hip software developer ("I can wear jeans to work, have a lip ring, shoot hoops at night") or starting a webzine because it is more in sync with their personal style, are also often authenticity-seekers.

Collegiality-seekers: "I need to work with people. I'm a people person." Collegiality-seekers associate strongly with their team or work group and derive much of their identity from belonging to it. They are extremely loyal to whatever group they belong to. Fun for them is going out for a drink after work with other members of the group. They welcome signifiers of their group membership, whether a photo of the team or a plaque commemorating a particular project.

Members of this group regard careers as important, but when asked what is most important they usually say it is working with people they enjoy. As one woman manager who had just recently moved into a new job from a role as an independent consultant put it, "I need to have a tribe."

Although collegiality-seekers are often attracted to working for large organizations, they may also choose to work in smaller firms, so long as their needs for affiliation are met. Unlike their independent-thinking or entrepreneurial counterparts, this group loves the team-building events that take place at off-site meetings. They are not happy working by themselves. As a general rule they are not drawn to telecommuting.

Many contract workers who are collegiality-seekers complain about the lack of belonging they experience going from contract to contract. Unfortunately, as independent work becomes the norm for them — whether as project workers, contractors, or independent consultants — these "people-persons" may be disadvantaged.

Tailoring Rewards

Savvy employers can take advantage of understanding the different types of new worker by tailoring rewards and systems to reflect different motivations. They need to offer a variety of options, such as additional vacation time, flexible time to accommodate caring for elderly parents, money to attend a conference, or the opportunity to own a high-profile project. In this way, employers will be able to individualize rewards and meet the broad range of preferences that characterize the new worker.

The New Worker

Type	**Motivation**
Independent Thinkers/Entrepreneurs	Autonomy
Lifestylers	Flexibility
Personal Developers	Learning/Growth
Careerists	Advancement
Authenticity-Seekers	Self-Expression
Collegiality-Seekers	Belonging/Loyalty to Team

Career-Defining
Moments

*W*hen Carol received her performance appraisal, her boss told her, "You're doing outstanding work – with a little more seasoning, you'll be an excellent candidate for my job."

Carol was surprised at her own response. "I knew I should feel flattered and excited. But I just felt flat. I had always *assumed* that this was what I wanted, but once it became a reality, I realized that it wasn't what I wanted at all. It would be more of the same, only with more headaches."

Ted, a 50-something professional with his own practice, got a letter from his building's management company offering him a 10-year lease renewal on his office suite. "Suddenly I found myself asking, am I really going to be doing this for another 10 years?"

Most of us don't spend a lot of time thinking about our future lives and careers. We are busy enough just keeping our show on the road, doing, working. And there may also be the nagging, largely unacknowledged fear that if we looked too hard at what we are doing now, we might not like what we saw. Most of us just keep on keeping on. Until, like Carol or Ted, we hit one of life's *career-defining moments*.

A career-defining moment is one that forces us to take stock of where we are right now, and where we want to go in the future. It's a sense of having reached a kind of crossroads – a moment of decision as to our future paths.

Sometimes a career-defining moment is a dramatic incident that jars us out of our well-worn ruts: we lose a job, a close friend battles a life-threatening illness, we win the lottery. But just as often, it emerges from a relatively ordinary life situation, like Carol's performance review.

A career-defining moment is, typically, a signal that you need to change your course – or at the very least, sit down and think very carefully about your future.

At different times in our lives, most of us find ourselves doing work that is in some way wrong for us, from taking a job we really don't want, because it will "round out our résumé," to doing work that is mind-numbingly dull because we can't galvanize ourselves to seek out something better. For whatever reason, we lose the plot. Our work is out of line with our values and priorities, or else it lacks meaning and purpose for us. It is then that we are ripe for a career-defining moment.

Of course, such a moment need not lead us to change our lives. We can always ignore it, and hope it goes away. Ralph, a commercial lawyer, had a career-defining epiphany early in his career. "I saw that the only difference between what I was doing now and what I would be doing in 20 years was that the deals would be bigger and the consequences of error would be more severe. But otherwise I would be doing exactly the same thing."

Ralph, however, chose to ignore that insight. He has continued to practice the same kind of law, consciously trading-off the tedium of repetition against the status and monetary rewards his work offers him. In this he is no different from many other professionals who are similarly bored with the repetitiveness of their work, from CAs to management consultants to doctors. "Whoever said work was *supposed* to be fun?" Ralph asks.

Often, as in Ralph's case, failure to embrace a career-defining moment stems from a streak of Puritanism. So what if we're unhappy and dissatisfied with our work? Life is tough, we tell ourselves. Get over it. Don't be so indulgent. Stop taking your emotional temperature.

We may be sceptical, too, about our ability to reinvent our lives, asking, "What if I try to do something different, and I fail? I don't want to look like a pathetic wannabe." Feeling unequal to the challenge, we retreat instead into what we know, to the secure and predictable.

Often, we exaggerate the consequences of trying and failing. Old scripts, particularly ideas about our financial needs, may hold us back.

Sally, for example, was part of the management team of a company that was taken over. She received a large lump sum on being let go. At first, she felt a great sense of release. She had been bored with her work for some years, and this was a perfect opportunity to get into a business she had long dreamed of, designing and leading eco-tours. It was a venture that would bring together her love and knowledge of travel and fitness. But on second thought, she was afraid this was too risky. Perhaps she should simply look for another job.

After sitting down with her financial planner, Sally realized that she was being overcautious. Her house was paid for, her children had finished university, she had considerable savings. Even if her business venture failed, she would still have food on her table and a roof over her head. She could afford to take a chance.

Change is always scary. Reinventing yourself and your life always involves some risks. It's important to carefully examine the possible tradeoffs involved. But you shouldn't underestimate your own capacity to rise to the occasion, or to find the internal resources that will allow you to withstand setbacks and overcome obstacles.

So when you feel a career-defining moment, don't try to shrug it off. Instead, embrace it, and let it show you where you want to go.

Who Will Win?

Introverts vs. Extroverts

Carolyn L. is an independent management consultant who makes her living giving speeches and delivering workshops and seminars. Many people who know her think of her as being sociable and outgoing. They also consider her the consummate networker, with her Filofax full of business contacts and professional associates. And in fact if you knew her only through her work, you would probably describe her as socially highly skilled. Despite such appearances, Carolyn insists that she is actually an extreme introvert.

"When I'm giving a workshop," she says, "I always arrive just before it starts, so I don't have to stand around making small talk. And when I'm finished I don't linger to mingle, but get away as soon as possible. I rarely attend professional network events, and when I go to parties I never stay long. And perhaps most telling of all, I never have business lunches and I don't carry business cards."

The concepts of introversion and extroversion have become part of our everyday vocabulary. Parents, in describing the personality characteristics of their children, will label them as "shy" or "outgoing." In fact, one of the first distinguishing characteristics we invoke in describing what "someone is like" is their sociability: the extent to which they are friendly and outgoing.

Who Is More Successful?

There is still a lot of misunderstanding about the personality characteristics of introversion and extroversion, despite the efforts of psychologists like Carl Jung and H. J. Eysenck to explain the concept, and despite the remarkable popularity of the Myers-Briggs Type Indicator, which assesses these attributes, among others (and which has become as much a cornerstone of corporate life as the personal computer).

Typically, we equate social skill with extroversion so that we tend to think of people as being either social skilled extroverts or emotionally klutzy introverts. And because of the apparent connection to social skills, we attribute all kinds of other positive characteristics to extroverts, such as warmth, friendliness, authoritativeness . . . in essence, success. By the same token, we ascribe negative characteristics to introverts: they are withdrawn, quiet, passive, "won't set the world on fire."

And historically, at least, it has been the *apparent* extroverts who have been most valued in business circles for their ability to mix easily, establish relationships, put people at their ease, and facilitate team-building, all key attributes for success in managers. Indeed, when I ask people in workshops whether they believe there is a connection between leadership and sociability, they typically describe their senior managers as being extroverted. After all, being a leader means that you have to be "good with people" – the implication being that introverts are *not* good with people. This attitude is reflected in executive searches where the word "outgoing" is commonly used as an adjective for "leader."

Actually, this is a rather simplistic set of assumptions. The fact is that both introverts and extroverts can be "good with people," depending on the circumstances. Many introverts like Carolyn are extremely effective and successful in business. Their interpersonal success, however, is a function of *situational* characteristics, that is, the degree to which the situation is structured and task-focused or unstructured and open-ended.

For example, if you bumped into Carolyn on the street, you might think that she was awkward, standoffish, even arrogant, though in fact she is simply shy. (Nine times out of ten, when I hear people described as "arrogant," I know that they are probably shy or uncomfortable in social situations.) But in a more structured situation such as a workshop, with a clear purpose and set of objectives to be accomplished, Carolyn shines.

Indeed, when we look at senior managers, we see that very few of them are in fact extroverted. Most are in the middle of the scale (so-called "ambiverts") or on the introverted side. Being friendly and outgoing can only carry you so far. Typically, in order to achieve a senior-management position, you not only need to be able to establish relationships quickly and relate to diverse kinds of people, you also have to spend considerable time by yourself behind closed doors, thinking and planning. (Notable exceptions to this are senior managers in customer-service environments such as hotels, stores, and retail banks, where a significant aspect of management is accomplished by "walking around.")

Are you more extroverted or introverted? Do you get your energy from being around other people? Or do you prefer to spend time working by yourself? How comfortable are you in teamwork environments? Does an open-office concept energize you — there is always someone you can relate to. Or does it depress you — no privacy, you can't hear yourself think, there is always someone bothering you.

The answer to these questions could have significant implications for everything from your choice of work setting to your preferred style of learning (extroverts thrive in a classroom setting with lots of opportunity for discussion, while introverts are comfortable spending time by themselves quietly hitting the books).

Indeed, I am often surprised at how little thought people give to understanding their own sociability, how defensive they become when it is suggested they are more introverted than extroverted, and how little attention they pay to their own sociability in making important career choices.

John P., for example, was happy as a marketing manager in a field office, heading up a successful sales team. It was a noisy environment with a lot of social interaction and spontaneous meetings. The team was close-knit and often would end the day going to a bar together or to someone's house for an impromptu barbecue.

John was then moved to head office to examine the feasibility of introducing a new product. Now he spends most of his time doing research on the Internet, reading reports, and crunching numbers on a computer terminal, and he is miserable. Although he has all the technical skills to handle his new assignment, he is unable to function effectively in a work environment that provides so little interaction with people. John is now thinking about making a career move. With a little more insight into his own personality, he could have avoided this situation in the first place.

Understanding your own preference can also help you in your relations with colleagues and others you work with. For example, Bill, an extremely gregarious vice-president of human resources, liked to drop by the office of Susan, his training director, whenever he was working on a report – to "talk it out." Susan, an introvert, found these unplanned meetings extremely irritating. "Can't he do anything himself? Do we have to live out of each others' pockets?" she complained. Bill's reaction? That Susan was rigid, abrupt, and "uptight." Developing an appreciation for each other's preferred way of working led to a significant improvement in their relationship.

Leveraging Your Own Style

A little self-knowledge can also help you successfully navigate in today's emerging new workplace. That workplace is characterized by *temporariness*. Work is increasingly organized around teams that coalesce around a particular project and then dissolve once its objectives have been achieved. Some people work on these projects as full-time employees, some as part-time or contract staff, some as independent contractors, but all share the same need to market themselves for new assignments once the current project is over.

So who will be more successful? At first glance, extroverts might appear to be at an advantage in this freewheeling economy. Whether as employees or independent contractors, they would seem better able to network their way into the best projects, to work effectively in teams, to establish relationships with a broad range of people, and to market themselves effectively for new positions or contracts.

And yet, on closer examination, the picture may not be quite so one-sided. One of the paradoxes of the new workplace is that while you need the ability to work in groups, you also need the discipline to work by yourself, whether at home, in the office or on an airplane. Indeed, with the pressure to reduce office overhead and to meet people's needs for more flexible hours, many people find themselves spending more time working from home or on the road. Moreover, many types of work are increasingly being outsourced to independent consultants who work alone much of the time, often from their homes. For extroverts, who get their energy from others, working this way can be uncomfortable and dispiriting. One frequently hears about people who left corporate life to set up their businesses only to discover that they are extremely lonely and miss the collegiality of the office.

Introverts, on the other hand, may actually prefer the more temporary and superficial working relationships that characterize today's projects. They don't need to *bond* with anyone to get the work done. And in today's task-focused, get-to-the-point-quickly business culture this can be an asset.

And while they may be at an initial disadvantage when it comes to networking and selling themselves in the more traditional manner, introverts can still be successful if they can develop marketing strategies that suit their personalities.

I know a number of highly successful consultants who have established their professional credentials by making presentations at conferences, writing articles for professional journals, becoming media commentators. In other words, they have established themselves as experts in their field, so although they may be seen as short on "schmooze," they are high on knowledge and credibility.

Indeed, with sufficient effort, introverts can become more effective marketers than many extroverts – particularly the ones who confuse having lunch with people and collecting business cards with the meaningful exchange of information that will establish your credentials or help sell business. (One of the most common mistakes independently employed extroverts make is to confuse the number of social interactions they have with live business potential.)

By the same token, extroverts can develop strategies to compensate for their own difficulties in the new workplace. For example, some chatty extroverts say that they had to learn how to repress their natural desire to establish *personal* relationships with people with small talk before a meeting begins, or to go off on interesting tangents in the meeting itself.

Extroverts can also work happily and successfully as independent contractors, so long as they build regular social contact with clients, associates, and professional colleagues into their daily schedules. Other common strategies include joining professional associations, establishing weekly lunches or workouts at the gym with a friend, setting up brainstorming sessions with colleagues and customers.

Some will achieve this by finding a business partner – a good idea so long as it doesn't result in *two* unemployed consultants sitting around schmoozing rather than seeking contracts. (Unfortunately, there is a tendency for extroverts to be attracted to extroverts and introverts to be attracted to introverts instead of seeking out a partner who will offset weaknesses.)

Both introverts and extroverts, then, can thrive in the new workplace. The key to doing so will be *self-knowledge* — understanding the environments in which you will excel. Work is elastic: it can take many shapes and forms. The trick will be not just finding but also *shaping* work to play to your own strengths and preferences. That will mean looking beyond the received wisdom — that says, for example, that the only way to market yourself and your services is to attend every possible network event and to "schmooze" with everyone and anyone you can. The challenge then is to find new ways to reach the same objectives. If you understand yourself, you will be able to achieve them your way.

20-Something
Career Angst

"I look at bios of successful people and they've done far more than me by this stage of their lives. These past few years are the time people really get the kind of credentials and experiences that look great on their résumé and last them a lifetime. And what have I accomplished? Basically I've blown it . . ."

— DANNY J., 26-YEAR-OLD STUDENT

*D*anny was everyone's golden boy — high-school valedictorian, winner of scholarships to top universities, college football star, straight-A student. But after completing a master's degree in economics, Danny's effortless progress began to falter. He enrolled in a doctoral program in political science, but dropped out after six months: it just didn't seem to be what he wanted to do. He enrolled in law school, but that didn't feel right, either. Now he's contemplating an MBA. He's interested in business, and he has the analytical skills employers are looking for. But he's really not sure.

"What if I'm wrong again?" Danny asks. "If I make another mistake, I'll just fall that much further behind the eight-ball. I look at my friends who went straight into professional schools such as law or computer science or whatever, and they're doing great. But I still don't know what I want to do. I really should *know* by now."

Moreover, like many perpetual students, Danny is guilt-ridden about accepting any further financial help from his parents. Worse, he's worried about disappointing them yet again. He feels under pressure — whether real or imagined — from them and from others to grow up, get a career, and get it *right* this time. Terrified of making any commitment, Danny marks time as an office temp, profoundly confused and depressed.

Danny is suffering from 20-something career angst — something I see a lot of these days:

> *"Should I go for my doctorate, or start earning big money right now?"*
> *"Should I stay with a big public accounting firm or get a job in industry?"*
> *"What kind of work would really suit me?"*
> *"What should I be when I grow up?"*

Twenty-somethings, of course, are not the only demographic group prone to such angst. But they are particularly vulnerable to it. And it must be admitted that people in their 20s have *always* been prone to career confusion and indecision. If you had asked me when I was that age what I wanted to do I would have said, "I don't have a clue." Like Danny I was troubled that I did not have a clear sense of direction. I was also convinced that that meant there was something wrong with me, and that everyone else had it more "together" than I did. I was envious of friends who seemed more certain about their own eventual place in the world. It was only later that I came to realize that few people are as certain as they appear, and in fact, most of my friends were just as confused as I was: they just didn't talk about it.

But if 20-something career angst is not new, it is certainly more pronounced, and more intense, than ever. In today's fast-shifting economy, the stakes are much higher for early career individuals, the margin for error much slimmer. The cost of a university education has spiraled at a time when many parents are cash-strapped. The pressure is on early to make the "right" decision. Kids feel that ambling along, making it up as you go, is not an option.

Career Pressures

This anxiety is exacerbated by a heightened consciousness about careers. These days, college and university students are bombarded with career advice. Career centers are located right on the campus. Career planning is part of the core curriculum. Among the bestselling issues of newsstand magazines are the ones that feature cover stories on "where the hot jobs are." The clear implication is that you *should* know what you want to do when you grow up.

Moreover, with the exception of an elite group with in-demand skills, such as engineering and computer technology, 20-somethings face an extremely challenging job market. Whereas in the past organizations hired for potential, today they are more likely to seek new hires who can "hit the ground running" and deliver value *now*, rather than taking their time to learn the ropes.

The traditional effort-reward equation has changed, so that 20-somethings don't believe that the rewards – that is, challenging, well-paying work – will be there relative to their efforts. And they may be right. A recent report shows the earnings of men and women 18 to 24 have declined about 20% over the past 20 years, even among those who are university educated (*Globe and Mail*, July 29, 1998).

Moreover, the work landscape is shifting fast with new specialties appearing while old ones disappear. Managing your career in this new workplace requires both assessing your own skills and interests and evaluating a multiplicity of options to see where you might best fit in. Of course, for young people with limited or no work experience, making career decisions can present a real conundrum. And so many ask, "How do I know I'll like it if I haven't done it?"

Adding to this anxiety and confusion is the ambivalence that many 20-somethings feel about working for an organization. Having seen their parents make significant sacrifices in terms of their personal lives, working long hours and giving unswerving loyalty to their corporations only to be cast aside in the great downsizing purges of the past decade, they are hesitant to commit to follow in their footsteps.

It's not surprising, then, that so many 20-somethings are so frightened of making a bad career choice, and so anxious to make the "right" decision.

Fear of Career Commitment

There are a number of strategies that 20-somethings can use to manage their career anxiety. But first, I'd like to offer a word of advice to the *parents* of these Hamlets for hire: *Chill out.* Don't put so much pressure – or even the appearance of pressure – on your kids.

We live in a society where everything – and not the least, education – is assumed to have an end-product. As early as grade school we ask children, "What do you want to be when you grow up?" – as though they should already know and should be preparing themselves for a particular job right now. We shouldn't be surprised that children internalize these societal pressures to decide what they want to be. Or that, as young adults, unable to live up to those perceived pressures, they may become completely paralyzed, unable to decide anything.

For the 20-something individual wrestling with career angst, the starting point is to recognize that there's nothing wrong with not knowing what you want to do. *Don't overestimate the consequences of making a "mistake."*

Instead of chasing after that elusive "right" decision, recognize that there are many possible career paths. When you are 45 years old, you are not going to look back and say, "If only when I was 25 years old I had done A, B, and C." That decision may appear momentous in the present – all the more so if there are debts from student loans or parental pressures to contend with. But, in the long term, the decision will have little or no impact on prospects for successful participation in the work force.

The long term usually takes care of itself. Indeed, given the fast-changing nature of work and the accelerating shift towards an economy based on temporary employment, it makes little sense to try to plan out an entire career. Entering a workplace where even a "full-time" job may last only a few years, and work is increasingly done by contract workers and self-employed external suppliers, you should focus on building a portfolio of skills and experiences that will ensure longer-term employability. *There is no beginning line and no finish line* in careers – and no right or wrong time to pursue a particular career option.

In this context, every experience counts. Even bad work experiences, painful though they may be at the time, can be valuable and important. I know of few successful people who have not at one time or another had some really hideous work experience. It's simply part of growing up. And it's part of how we learn what we like and don't like.

Career angst is itself a painful kind of experience, full of indecision and soul-searching. Some people try to avoid this process by closing down their options. Rather than seeking work that will best match their interests and skills, they surrender to the marketplace and pursue some "hot" career path or other whether or not they are suited to it.

But if instead you engage with your career angst, and struggle with it, you will come out on the other side with a much clearer sense of your values and priorities, and a renewed commitment to career success.

"Hey 40-Something, I'm Talking to You!"

*H*ey 40-something, get a life! You're obsessed with work, you measure yourself by short-term, narrow-minded, quarterly results, you think exercise and work-life balance comes from hopping on a treadmill, you don't know your kids.

You talk about values, but you don't have the balls to actually live them. So don't bore me by trying to sell me on your value statements.

You hired me because you said you wanted outside-the-box thinking, but every time I make a suggestion, you look at me like I'm crazy. You don't really want outside-the-box thinking. You do the same things you've always done, or you change the color of the box and tell us all about it in a company-wide e-mail.

We sit around in endless meetings and talk about what's wrong and what needs to be done. You tell us you understand, yet after the meeting things stay the same. If you spent a little bit more time actually *doing* something – being bold, shaking things up – and worried less about office politics and the way things have always been, you might actually get somewhere.

You say that this workplace cares about young people, but if I want to live, dress, talk, or act like a young person, you can't handle it.

You hold yourself up as a model and call yourself my mentor. You tell me that when you were my age, you were prepared to put in your time and earn your own way. Think about this for a second: I'm way overqualified for this job. And the truth of the matter is that you wouldn't even have gotten this job with your skills and qualifications today. You think I'm impatient and not willing to wait my turn just because I want to do something meaningful with my time.

You say all we're interested in is money. That's a conceit. You guys jump for money, too — it's just that you end up getting it.

We live in different worlds. You complain about how big your mortgage is and how expensive private schools are. But it was you who got us into this spot — bidding up the price of housing, overburdening the social system — and yet you still ended up with the great career and the two cars. Now we have to have roommates to get by and spend all of our time marketing ourselves for the next contract.

You stuck me in this cubicle and gave me e-mail. I spend half my life sending messages to the friends I never see, and listening to the calls going on around me, trying not to tune in on the ones where my cube-mates are working out their relationships, whispering, "I can't talk now," and quietly hanging up the phone.

I know I've got a lot to offer — I'm creative, independent, technically savvy, and prepared to take risks. Unfortunately, you don't seem to know how to take advantage of those skills and you never take my new ideas seriously.

I'm prepared to kill myself for my projects, even if it means working my butt off for a month around the clock, but I expect something back.

Don't tell me I'm your most important resource, because if you really cared about me and my career, you would treat me like I'm more than just a unit of productivity and not just a leverage for your career.

P.S. Just because you ordered Starbucks roast for the coffee maker and put in recycling bins doesn't mean you understand.

"Hey 20-Something,
I'm Talking to You!"

*H*ey, 20-something, get real! You talk about how you are ideally suited to this new workplace because you grew up with a life on fast-forward – what do you think, I can't breathe and talk at the same time?

You think you've discovered independence and learning, like you're the first generation who was ever concerned about being challenged at work. You think you're so precious and unique, with your lattes (you didn't discover cafés), and your cute little shirts. But you're arrogant and you overestimate your qualifications. You may have knowledge in your head, but you have no experience.

You talk about office politics as if it's a contagious disease. Actually, it's how a lot of important information is exchanged and you can learn an awful lot about what's really going on.

You want everything to come easily to you and you want it now – high-profile projects, interesting work, contact with senior management. But you're never going to get ahead if you're not prepared to make some sacrifices, if you don't learn to play the game and what it takes to make a success of yourself in this organization.

You're not entitled to any damn thing except what you earn. The world is not going to offer you anything on a platter. You have a lot of potential, but you won't be able to realize it with this attitude. You need to learn to take a long-term view. You need to learn how to delay gratification, to pay your dues. You're not a kid anymore.

Your generation prides itself on its ability to take risks and deal with uncertainty. But ironically, you're always looking for guarantees that whatever you do is going to give you an immediate payoff, that it's going to lead to the right job or the right project or the right career path. Guess what — there are no guarantees. Getting ahead is not simply a question of following a formula and checking off the ingredients. You're never going to get the clarity or reassurance you're looking for.

And stop asking me for constant feedback. Sometimes I feel that you're always saying, "Feed me, stroke my ego." Of course you want to know how well you are doing. But you're not my only priority. And although I respect your need for feedback, sometimes you're going to have to live with either getting no feedback or waiting your turn.

You have no sense of the commitment I've made, or respect for anything that went on before you were here. You think everything was invented yesterday. You have no appreciation for the knowledge, wisdom, and know-how we have accumulated over the years, and trust me, being able to deal with people and touchy issues is no different today than it ever was.

You talk about this workplace not being sympathetic to your style and values. Why should I design a special workplace just for you?

Do you have to be so cocky? I know you want to make a meaningful contribution, and I know your opinions are important, but there are some skills you need to develop before you will be seen as a serious player here.

Yes, we want to hire you, but don't hold me to ransom with your signing bonuses like we are so desperately in search of talent that we will do anything to court you.

You have no sense of loyalty. All you care about is money. You would jump ship for an extra few dollars. You don't understand how to weigh up money relative to the kind of skills and opportunities you can get here. Balancing your work and personal life is all you ever talk about – your marathons, your time with friends. What, you don't think I care about my family, that I don't have a life?

P.S. I'm really sick of hearing how your generation is so much better adapted to the workplace because of your use of technology. Yes, I know how to work with new technology, I can use a computer, can multitask, and can take risks. But there is nothing wrong with being a team-player or being able to spell.

"Hey 20-Something/
40-Something, Shut Up Already!"

I'm tired of you boomers thinking you define the world, and I'm sick of hearing how hip and happening you 20-somethings are. I'm 35 and I can't wait around forever. When does my big career start? Why can't we have our shot at the brass ring, too?

Our problem? We grew up with all the big expectations for the big jobs, the big careers. But we just got there a little bit too late. You boomers got the great careers and the great houses. All we got were two huge recessions and your dregs. Instead of the big houses, the housettes; instead of the big jobs, the jobettes; instead of the luxury sports utilities, the minivans. I'm sick of my two-hour commute to a sterile subdivision in the middle of nowhere, being forced to live in the middle of beyond just to make ends meet. But you're not about to retire tomorrow, so please don't tell me to wait my turn.

Every time I pick up the newspaper I read about some hip young entrepreneur making millions on the net, doing something "cool" with a hot new webzine, or developing a line of street clothing, because "it came out of my culture." And now organizations want to hire young talent because of their voice. Don't you think I have a voice, too?

We're the ones paying the price for boomer excesses. When we arrived in the job market in the late '80s and early '90s there were no jobs. Everyone was downsizing. We couldn't even get unpaid internships. We missed out on all the opportunities to get ahead. So we traveled, or went back to school, just to do something.

Now I'm doing the same job that people who are younger and much less experienced are doing. And everyone wants to hire 20-somethings, because they're cheaper and organizations think they're more current and more flexible – more easily molded into the company's image. So they have them leapfrogging ahead of me even though I've got way more experience.

Stuck in the middle with you – that's how I always feel. I look above me and see a big pampered mass of boomers complaining about their investments and I look behind me and I see a whole bunch of self-consciously precious 20-somethings nibbling at my backside, who don't think I'm prepared to take risks. I *am* prepared to take risks, but I also want security. Wait till you have kids. Security will be important to you, too.

And both you guys, you 20-somethings with no kids and you 40-somethings with teenagers, can't you figure out a way to schedule important meetings that takes into account that I've got a young family and baby-sitting responsibilities? No, I'm not prepared to pull a whole bunch of all-nighters – are you going to look after my kids?

Sure I want the big jobs, the promotions, this is what I was brought up to expect. But I also want challenge and learning. When I look at a job, my first question is, how will this add to my résumé or my portfolio of skills? Not, "Will it lead to a promotion?" Unlike my boomer bosses I don't see my job as a lifetime commitment but as a short-term engagement. Work to me is a means to an end, not an end in itself. But I'm also capable of lots of loyalty.

I feel squeezed on all fronts, like the proverbial middle kid. Our generation wasn't sexy enough to be endlessly profiled or hip enough to be courted for its style and pluckiness.

So here I am, expected to be a good parent, spend time with my kids, go to the school and run interference with the teachers. And at the same time, I have 5,000 competing priorities at work. So the work isn't getting done the way I want it, and by the time I get home I'm so wiped I have nothing left for my kids, much less my partner. A personal life? I barely get through the day. Excuse me if sometimes I seem a little bit tired or sour.

So 20-somethings, could you please shut up about how our workplace isn't cool enough, and how sick you are of going from contract to contract? At least you *have* work, and the opportunity to get some great experience. And 40-somethings, stop whining about how you'll never have enough money to retire. No one told you to spend so much money and get so much in debt.

P.S. We're the real Generation X – the anonymous generation nobody notices or cares about, with no identity of our own. You can look it up if you like (in Douglas Coupland's *Generation X: Tales for an Accelerated Culture*).

What 20-Somethings
Ask About Work and Careers

I started my organizational career doing career counseling for young professionals at a large petrochemical company in the late 1970s. The most common questions I was asked was: "What do I have to do to become vice-president in the next five years?" and "I've been offered a promotion which involves a transfer to Pipsypoo — will my career be dead-ended if I refuse?"

These days, I deliver many career-planning workshops to young professionals. Their questions are for the most part very different. They ask fewer questions about advancement and career-limiting moves. Here are the questions I am asked most frequently.

If you're a 40-something, understand what is on the hearts and minds of your young staff. You may discover that many of these concerns are not that different from those you once grappled with. And if you're in your 20s, or even your 30s, look at these questions relative to your own questions about your career and your life.

1. I have devoted all this time and money to pursuing a particular professional course. What if I've made a mistake? With so many career possibilities, how do I know if this is really right for me?

This is an existential question – and one of the questions I'm most frequently asked. With career choices, much as in the choice of a house or partner, you can never be absolutely certain that there isn't something better out there.

This kind of doubt and second-guessing is hardly unique to 20-somethings. Still, with the stakes so high, this generation has a greater fear of making a "career mistake" than their predecessors. When boomers entered the workforce it seemed that there was an endless amount of opportunity. If things didn't work out, you could always "go across the street" and get another job. Today, people don't feel they have that luxury – the bar for participation in the good life has moved into the stratosphere. And so they worry that if they take the wrong job they will be left even further behind the eight-ball.

Often, people seem to believe that there is one *perfect job* out there for them. In fact, there is no magic bullet, no one perfect job. Some matches are simply better than others. Very few people know what kind of work will represent a good fit for them until they actually *do* it, so there is often a period of trial and error. If you do end up in a job that is a bad match, that's not such a tragedy. The worst thing that can happen is that you will learn more about what is important to you in your working environment, and will be able to use that knowledge to make future career decisions.

In the meantime, you can significantly increase the likelihood of finding work that is a good match for you by gaining a clear sense of your own skills and interests and using this information to evaluate opportunities presented to you. For example, if you know you need a lot of autonomy, and get impatient with office politics, then in your job interviews ask targeted questions relating to those subjects. Discover how decisions get made (will you be endlessly second-guessed?) and how much freedom you will have on the job (will you be endlessly micromanaged?). Is this the type of environment where everything is done in teams and by consensus, or is there latitude for individual decision-making?

The good news is that most people do end up making decisions that put them on the right professional course. Trust yourself.

2. I left my previous job because my boss was a jerk. How do I explain this in job interviews?

Without savaging your former boss, talk about how you had fundamental differences in the way you viewed the work. Most employers are sensitive today about person-job match issues. They understand that in one environment you may experience difficulties because of what is often referred to as "personal chemistry," but in another you may thrive.

You would be surprised at how many people leave jobs because of a serious conflict with the boss. They may love the work content, and the organization, but over time a boss who is a jerk will take a significant toll on self-esteem and attitudes towards work – especially when it occurs early in your career.

An interviewer may grill you about the circumstances of your parting. Show how you tried to solve the problems when they occurred. Personally, I think people who leave an unhappy work situation are demonstrating emotional maturity and a strong belief in their own marketability.

3. Should I take a job I don't want just to make some money?

There's no problem with this, particularly if you have serious financial obligations to meet. While the work may not, at first blush, rate highly in terms of being challenging or personally meaningful for you, all experience counts.

At the same time, consider the opportunity costs. Taking a job that does not relate to your personal interests, or the skills you want to acquire at this stage of your career, may lead to your missing out on better opportunities that you could have found by devoting yourself to a more rigorous job search.

4. When they hired me they said they were looking for outside-the-box thinking. But every time I express an opinion, they basically tell me to shut up. Are there any organizations out there which really mean what they say and will treat me like I've got something to contribute?

At a recent meeting of senior human-resource professionals, a 28-year-old with multiple degrees complained that although she had been hired because of her educational credentials, she was basically doing clerical work. There was widespread agreement in the meeting that many of the larger and more traditional organizations in this country talk a good line but have failed miserably to actually follow through in using the extraordinary talents of the 20-somethings.

As a general rule you will have greater opportunities to have a direct impact on the business in smaller, more flexible organizations, younger industries such as high-tech and entertainment, and startup environments. Larger organizations can provide meaningful opportunities for contribution when each division is organized as if it is an independent company or autonomous work unit.

5. Where can I find a 35-hour-a-week job with good benefits and security?

Nowhere. The reality is that no job today is completely secure. Even so-called traditionally secure environments like government and health care have been rocked by productivity pressures, downsizing, and restructuring.

In fact, as mentioned above, today we all have to think of ourselves as temp workers, whether we have a so-called traditional job governed by the traditional employment contract or whether we are temporary, contingent, or contract workers.

A full-time position may not be any more secure than temporary work, but it does typically offer some kind of benefits package. Many companies now provide a menu of benefits that allows employees to tailor their own package based on their personal circumstances. Single people, for example, can drop family dental care coverage or life insurance in favor of vision care benefits or access to Employee Assistance Programs.

As for a 35-hour work week – dream on! Few salaried jobs involve less than 40 hours per week, with most people routinely putting in 50 hours and some up to 60 or 70.

6. My boss doesn't have a life. Does that mean I can't have one either?

Being able to balance work and personal life has become a critical workplace issue. Increasingly, in evaluating work opportunities people are putting personal time and having a life on the table as a key ingredient in negotiations.

There is, however, a significant generational difference in expectations of just exactly what an appropriate work week is and the importance of balancing work and personal life.

Forty-something bosses say: "Get real. All my 20-something staff care about is whether they'll be able to run in a marathon or leave work at six to meet their friends. When I was their age, if the boss asked me to work late, I did. After all, that was what was expected of me."

Twenty-something staff say: "Don't hold yourself up as a model. You're out of shape, you never see your family, and your boss still doesn't appreciate you."

Your boss came from a generation which believed there was a strong link between hard work and fast promotion up the corporate ladder. Today, the effort-reward equation has changed, but the boomers have not changed their expectations, of themselves and others around them.

Within this context, it's your responsibility to manage your boss. Without being unrealistic, make it clear what you are prepared to give up in personal time, and what you will not bend on. For example, you may need to pull a few all-nighters to get a project in on deadline, but it is reasonable to expect some personal time in return. If your boss still doesn't "get it" and you don't feel that the effort-reward equation justifies the excessive demands, then start looking for other work. You can't enjoy your job or be an effective contributor if you resent being there.

7. I've been offered a promotion to a managerial role at my company, but I'm not convinced that it's right for me. After hearing what the job involves, I'm worried that it's going to take me away from doing the type of projects I really love to do.

Your concern is that if you turn down this promotion, you will not be seen as being ambitious. Not too long ago, people would have thought you were crazy to turn down more responsibility, the money that goes with it, and the opportunity to advance your career. Today there is more appreciation of people who are thoughtful in choosing to do the kind of work that suits them and plays to their strengths. In other words, there's no longer the knee-jerk reaction that a promotion is good and you should automatically take it.

You may also prefer to play more of a specialist role than a role in management. Unfortunately, higher-level positions typically do involve managerial responsibilities. Be frank with your boss about your concerns. They may be able to modify the position to give you a better blend of professional and leadership responsibilities.

8. Why should I kill myself in this job? There's no place to go in this organization, and even if I do make a superhuman effort, no one seems to notice.

Actually, you'd be surprised at how much people do notice. The problem is, most people are too busy, pressured, and self-absorbed themselves to acknowledge the extra efforts of others. Also, consider the consequences of doing poor work. Today the expectation is that everyone will be working at 100%. You can be sure if you're not pulling your weight you will be noticed.

While we all want external confirmation – being noticed and thanked for a job well done – defining your value in those terms ultimately is very limiting. You need to be able to reward yourself by monitoring your accomplishments and taking credit where it's due, rather than relying on others for feedback. Don't be shy about tooting your own horn. Keep people you work with informed of your achievements and how you have added value to the work. Ensure you are producing the kind of work you can be proud of – that's what usually gets people noticed – work that, perhaps more importantly, gives you a sense that what you are doing is significant and worthy of celebration.

9. I've been offered a job in an organization I'm really interested in working for in the long term but I know my circumstances will change in the short term (I'm planning to go to Europe to study Italian/to start a family/to take time off to finish my Ph.D. thesis). Should I take the job here knowing that I'm not going to stay and risk pissing them off?

As John Lennon observed, life is what happens when you're making other plans. The world rarely unfolds the way we expect it to. You may have plans to get pregnant, or take a trip, but obviously things beyond our control are also at work. Rather than worrying about what would happen if you left in the near future, think about the learning experiences you would be losing by not working for this organization and the missed opportunity to demonstrate your value.

Organizations are made up of human beings who understand that life is unpredictable. If you decide to leave for a personal reason, they probably will not hold your job until you return. But if you are doing an outstanding job, you are definitely in a privileged position among job seekers when you get back into the workforce. If nothing else, you have developed marketable skills and have established good contacts for the future.

Women in this situation who are planning to have children often worry that people will assume they have only taken the job to collect maternity benefits. Bear in mind that it may take years to get pregnant, you will likely be able to work throughout your pregnancy, and you can't possibly know now whether you will want to return to work after the baby is born anyway. So take the opportunity to get some experience and demonstrate your value when you have it.

10. In the future, who will be more in demand, specialists or generalists?

This is no longer a black-and-white dichotomy. The question today is really: Should I be *more* of a specialist or *more* of a generalist? So-called specialist work is usually tied to a particular professional area, for example environmental law, forensic accounting, or computer-based animation. Generalist work typically requires the use of a broader range of skills such as managing projects, coordinating resources, and implementing programs.

Today, of course, everyone needs such general skills as being a good team member, giving effective presentations, being able to establish credibility, working under pressure, and so on.

If you choose the specialist route, you will need both depth and breadth of knowledge at a very elite level. If you cannot say, "I am among the best people in my field in this city/country," this is not the route for you.

Remember also that the demand for specialists changes with technology, world events, environmental regulations, and so on, so *don't give up on your generalist skills*. Be sure to have a fall-back position.

On the other hand, the demand for generalists – people who can work with others from a broad range of disciplines – will increase as the world becomes increasingly complex. That said, you still need something to give you a competitive edge, professional expertise to "hang your hat on" – be it a good understanding of biomechanics, marketing, agribusiness, or something else.

11. I've been trained as an engineer/accountant/lawyer. I don't want to be limited to that role. How can I branch out into other areas?

This is one of the most common concerns I hear from young professionals who worry about being stereotyped. No sooner do they receive their professional designation, be it in law, engineering, or accounting, than they decide they really want to do something else.

In today's highly competitive job market, there is an easy way to change disciplines when you are starting out. Establish your skills and demonstrate your value to the enterprise in the area in which it is easiest to secure employment by virtue of your professional credentials. This is good advice whether you are an accountant who wants to move out of finance into marketing, or a lawyer who wants to move into communications. In other words, demonstrate your generalist skills to your employer before trying to compete with marketing professionals who hold specialized degrees in that area. You can then leverage the skills and experiences you have acquired to move into other areas.

One woman, after a short stint as a lawyer, parlayed her background in law into a career in journalism specializing in legal issues. Another lawyer used problem-solving and analytical skills to become a systems consultant.

A third combined her curiosity about people, her appreciation of individual differences, and her broad professional network to move into executive recruitment.

12. Do I need to do a lot of research on the job market? Can't I just go to a headhunter?

A headhunter is hired and paid for by companies looking for job candidates. You may want to approach a search firm that specializes in your field to increase your odds of getting interviewed by organizations you'd like to work for. But remember, recruiters do not necessarily have your interests at heart. They are not career counselors. They don't work for you, and it's not their job to find the best match for you. And they can only interview you for spots they have been hired to fill if your qualifications fit.

By all means talk to headhunters – but only as part of a careful and thorough job search of your own. Be aware also that, as a general rule, headhunters work at more senior levels, focusing on seasoned workers, or in high-end specialties such as information technology.

13. Do I have to work on my birthday?

Regrettably, your birthday is not a public holiday. Unless you choose to take it as a vacation day or a personal day, you will almost certainly have to work. Very few organizations have a policy of allowing their employees to take their birthdays off (although it's a nice idea).

14. If I'm called for an interview for something I'm really not interested in, should I go?

Yes. It's an opportunity to hone your interviewing skills, as well as to learn about another industry or type of work. Even if the job doesn't appear to interest you, you may be surprised and find that the job is a better match than you thought. You also don't know where the interview may lead, as the interviewer may well identify other opportunities that could prove more suitable.

15. I really want to travel for a while. Will a year off look bad on my résumé?

There used to be much more rigid ideas about what looked good or bad on a résumé – and periods of non-gainful employment were definitely considered bad. In the new work environment, however, we have very different concepts about what employment continuity means. It used to be that people would go to school, then maybe "take a year off" and go travel in Europe, and then get down to the serious business of earning a living – all in a more or less linear fashion, with an expected and predictable linear professional progression. The path today is far less straightforward.

Essentially, we are all working in what I have called TempWorld. Work life will consist of a series of short-term assignments and we will be constantly moving back and forth between different life domains, whether it be travel, work, family, recreation, and education, without any rigid boundaries between them. As such it no longer makes sense to talk about the idea of taking a year off as if that year has no value.

In a fast-changing global economy, independence, the capacity to take risks, self-management skills, and experience and knowledge of other cultures will be highly valued – precisely the behaviors and skills you will acquire in your adventure.

16. Should I do an MBA?

Pursue a higher-level business degree – for that matter any degree – only if it will help you achieve your *personal* goals. Don't undertake any kind of education simply because it's a "hot" professional qualification, or will give you entry to an area where you think the jobs will be in the future. In the long run, your time would have been better invested in upgrading your education in an area of personal interest.

The perceived value and demand for MBAs is extremely cyclical. Some years they are all the rage, while a few years later, employers are saying that people with the degrees are great with the spreadsheets but lack the creativity and depth of thought we need. You shouldn't pursue something just because you think that's what the market wants you to do.

17. What are the "hot" skills or occupations?

I'm not a great fan of preparing for the future by trying to second-guess where the hot occupations will be. I call it the "top 10" or "what's hot/what's not" approach to career planning. What's hot today can well be rendered meaningless tomorrow by any number of factors such as global events, the Asian flu, changes in government policy, and new technology. In fact, if you were to look at a list of what are currently considered hot jobs, you probably couldn't pronounce half of them, much less know what they are. Hot jobs change almost as fast as the weather.

Still, you can take advantage of business trends. For example, looking into the future we know that environment issues will continue to grow in importance. Similarly, as society continues to cut back on spending in the public health sector, anything that keeps people healthier longer will be a winner, as will anything that combines technology with biology. In an age of continuous learning combined with a generation weaned on media, being able to use the media to promote life-long learning in the field known as edutainment will be a hot area. Finally, keep in mind that aging boomers are tired and jaded, and have a growing interest in the environment: anything that packages recreation and physical fitness with environmental awareness – be it hiking in the rainforest or birdwatching – will continue to grow in popularity.

When making career choices, know what you care about. Don't try to second-guess the marketplace. Identify your own personal passions and pursue them.

18. What are the hot or best companies to work for?

To some extent this is a matter of individual preference. To one person, "hot" may mean a company that's growing, doing a lot of R&D, and has lots of young people to shoot hoops with in the office. For another, it may mean great international opportunities and working with leading-edge technology. As a general rule, many young people today prefer smaller, more entrepreneurial organizations that are growing in so-called hot areas such as edutainment, biotechnology, and other high-tech industries.

But you can't really stereotype by size. For example, I do a lot of work with the large accounting firms, where there is tremendous opportunity – if, that is, you are interested in the areas where they are growing.

For many people, the best companies are the ones that offer more autonomy and the opportunity to really make a difference.

19. I love my work but have been offered more money elsewhere. Should I tell my boss or will she think I'm blackmailing her?

Talent is scarce and very expensive to replace. If the issue is really one of money and that is all it will take to keep you, then you should tell your boss, and make it very clear that you are not blackmailing her. Given the cost of hiring and training a replacement, she probably has a real interest in ensuring you stay put.

On the other hand, if you are jumping ship for just a few extra dollars, it may prove short-sighted in the long run. Ask yourself, is everything equal in both positions in terms of training and development opportunities, in terms of people you can really learn from? If the answer is no, you may be much better off where you are.

20. If I'm well-groomed, why can't I wear a lip ring?

Good question. Much of this is determined by organizational climate. Are you working in a more conservative environment, like financial services, or a creative one, like advertising? If your boss is saying you can't wear a lip ring because clients will react negatively, check out how realistic this perception is. Many baby boomer bosses are projecting onto younger generations their own beliefs about what's acceptable.

As one young person in advertising put it, "We went to make the call, and the client had a nose ring, a lip ring, and was dressed more like I wanted to look than the way my boss was dressed."

What it comes down to is, how much does this mean to you? How much will you have to sacrifice personally? Is this worth a confrontation?

21. I'm in a dead-end job. Should I quit? How can I make the most of my time here?

You may have to rethink what you mean by a "dead-end" job. Even so-called McJobs can provide opportunities for making significant accomplishments over and above the day-to-day work. It's up to you to be vigilant in identifying potential opportunities. Make the most of your time in your current position by thinking strategically about how you can use your skills at a higher level. Look for opportunities to add value – for example by finding a problem and solving it – and take advantage of every potential learning experience.

Another strategy you can use is "shadowing." Are there people in your work environment from whom you can learn? Ask your boss or other people whose work interests you if you can follow them around for the day or accompany them on an important assignment.

At this stage in your career, you should not be thinking of the prestige associated with your job title, but what experience you can get from the job. Think in terms of accomplishments that you can add to your résumé: for example, taking over a project from your supervisor, winning the employee-of-the-month award, or making an innovative suggestion for service delivery.

Finally, remember that you're not in prison. If your job isn't meeting your needs, look for better work.

22. How do I move up in this organization? No one seems to notice the work I'm doing, and I don't want to be at this level forever.

Today's organizations are flat, making the competition for higher level work much more intense. There are more people chasing fewer opportunities. Rather than getting caught up in the prestige associated with your title or the number of salary increases you have received, ask yourself a few questions. Are you learning on the job? Are you gaining skills? Are you improving your own employability? Those are the real measures of success. Measure your progress not by your promotions but by the content of your work. Is it increasing in complexity? Does it have more of an impact on the success of the enterprise?

23. Some people seem so comfortable passing out their business cards, calling up acquaintances, meeting people for lunch. But to me all this networking seems a little forced. I know I'm supposed to be constantly marketing my skills, but at what point is enough enough?

People vary in their attitudes towards networking and the degree to which they are comfortable networking. One reason some avoid it is that they worry that they will be seen as using people, or else think it means acting phony.

However, studies show that successful people actively cultivate and maintain broad networks. Rather than looking at networking as using people to "get them to do something for you," they think of it as being one of the many resources they use in managing their career and work — as, in this instance, a knowledge resource. Other people are vital stores of information and knowledge about how things get done, new ways of thinking about a problem, potential new clients, new ideas, new opportunities. Don't think purely in instrumental terms, evaluating the usefulness of a network member in terms of their ability to "pay off" by delivering a job lead or client contact. Think of yourself as developing mutually supportive relationships in which you may be helping someone who helps someone else, and eventually the favor returns to you.

Keep your network as broad as possible. Stay in touch with people you went to university with and former managers who can be an important source for references and work leads. (See Part IV for more on networking.)

24. I really hate office politics. Is there any workplace out there where being political isn't part of the package?

A lot of people say they don't like office politics, but as often as not the politics turns out simply to be different groups of people expressing different points of view and trying to influence each other or make them understand their opinions. In fact, this can be an extremely healthy and creative way to communicate. If, however, you are referring to a level of politics that is simply petty whining about personalities, you have control over your entry into the fray.

What is often thought to be negative about office politics is people venting and expressing their feelings. But in fact, we all need that kind of exchange where we are testing out our own feelings. For example, in an office where politics did not exist, you might find a whole group of people who feel that "there is something wrong with them" because they can't get along with their boss. Given the chance to compare notes with co-workers, they would realize the boss is actually insensitive and abusive.

Remember, office politics is often an important source of information about what is actually going on and can help keep you "tied in" to the decisions being made. Information picked up at meetings does not always tell the complete story. The nuances of people's motivations, feelings about what has been proposed – all this adds the real meat to information and helps you to know what is important and what isn't.

25. I'm sick of going from contract to contract and always having to sell myself, not having any money, and not being able to make any plans. Is there such a thing as a real job out there?

Sorry, Virginia, you will be hard pressed to find a "job" in the traditional sense of the word – something with security and a predictable pension. But that doesn't mean there isn't a lot of interesting and challenging work out there. Make sure your skills are up to date, that you have a skills portfolio that you could sell to other potential employers, and that you have money in the bank for any downtime.

If it's security that you crave, knowing that you are capable of managing your own career and selling your services to others will be your security.

26. Some of my friends have been offered signing bonuses. How do I get one?

You have to have a special set of skills in a profession where there is intense competition for talent. Signing bonuses were once offered only to senior executives to lure them away from one lucrative position to another. More recently they have been used to attract professionals in high-demand areas, such as information technology and edutainment, software development, and to reel in much-sought-after seasoned project managers.

If you are offered a signing bonus, be aware that it will probably come with strings attached. Your new employer will probably want you to stay with their company for two to three years to get their money's worth, and may prorate it over that period to ensure you do stick around.

Career-Development Tips for 20-Somethings

To summarize . . .

- Find a mentor — someone you can learn from.
- Look to increase your experience: "eavesdrop" in important meetings, leverage your skills, volunteer.
- Expand your skills portfolio.
- Shadow someone who is doing work that interests you.
- Pursue education at the highest broadest level.
- Increase your personal profile/network.
- Look at opportunities in terms of learning, not the effort-reward equation.
- Understand the mind-set of 40-something bosses.
- Recognize that there are no "right" career choices.

How to Career-Proof
Your Children

*E*lizabeth's 11-year-old son just returned home from summer camp, proudly proferring a gift: a hand-carved wooden duck. Elizabeth is concerned about this new and unexpected talent. "He used to say he was going to be a doctor," she says. "What if he wants to be a woodworker now?"

Doug arranged a summer job volunteering at a senior citizens home for his 14-year-old daughter — not because it was a good thing for her to do, but because "it will look good on her résumé."

Bob is sending his seven-year-old son to a summer camp that he really can't afford: "It's never too early to start making the right kind of contacts," he says.

"My kid didn't do anything this summer," complains Linda. "Next year it'll be time for him to get down to business and use his time more productively." Linda's son is 13.

Career Hypersensitivity

When parents start to apply the same productivity obsession to their children's summer activities as they do to their own work, you know that the world has changed. People have become so anxious and hyper-vigilant about the future that they take everything their children do and filter it through the template of future careers.

For example, a comment on a project that little Dougie is sometimes intolerant of his fellow team members is heard as "little Dougie is not a good team player and will never make it in a team-oriented work environment." Similarly, a report that Sally failed to take initiative in French class is interpreted as "Sally lacks leadership skills."

We have become obsessed with the new marketplace. It is telling, in this context, to see to whom parents and the media turn for career advice: senior industrial managers and leaders. We seek their advice about the future of work in this country, and how the educational system can better meet the needs of industry. Certainly, they have a handle on some of the challenges facing us. But just because someone understands a business plan doesn't mean she has an understanding of child and adolescent development, or the psychological process that underlies how people make career choices, or individual differences in temperament. Nor does she necessarily have any special insight into the future of work.

One of the most common questions I hear from senior managers is not about their staff's career concerns, or even their own, but about their children. They ask, "What should I tell my kids about careers? What advice and support should I give them?"

Parents have always been concerned about their children's future, and they have usually expressed some sort of expectations for what their children might accomplish. But never before have so many tried to micromanage every detail of their children's educational curriculum and career choices. There are good reasons, of course, for this level of concern. The stakes are so much higher. The world of work continues to change drastically. Many people have a hard time seeing where *they* will fit into the job picture a few years from now, let alone what will become of their children.

At the same time, the cost of post-secondary education has soared. It's not surprising that cash-strapped parents want to ensure that they are investing their dollars on the right program of study. They must also wrestle with a plethora of choices, between schools that specialize in science and technology and those that emphasize languages and arts; mainstream and alternative schools; public and private schools; community colleges and universities.

What About the Kids?

The result of this no-time-to-waste mentality is anxious, stressed-out kids overloaded with never-ending round of extracurricular activities (builds leadership and team-skills; broadens their skills base), jobs (résumé-building), and enrichment classes, to ensure they will make it among the "haves" in the future. Children are expected to decide early on their future careers, and then stick to that decision.

Indeed, in one much-lauded school board in California, high-school guidance counselors have an extremely sophisticated curriculum to help children make career choices as early as Grade 8 — and if they haven't decided by Grade 10, they get assistance from peer counselors.

One of the most common complaints I hear from parents about their teenage and post-teenage children is, "My kid isn't focused." These parents say their children can't make up their minds what programs they want to study or to what end, or keep changing university majors and are not using their time seriously.

I believe that it's a mistake to force children into premature career choices. Grade 9 or 10 is still too young to make decisions about the rest of your life. At this age, children are still too young to vote, they're supposed to call home if they're coming back late, and they haven't had sex yet (we hope) — so why should we expect them to know what they want to be doing at work when they're 40?

Children at this age will indeed often have ideas about what kind of work they might want to do. But they need some experience of the world of work before they can be clear about their skills, interests, and values, and where they will best fit in.

And after all, is the main challenge of childhood and adolescence to make our children future workers, ready to engage in the marketplace? I don't believe so. The main challenge should be to develop an interest in and curiosity about the world around us. Forcing kids to make premature career decisions only sets up a paradigm that the world is full of right or wrong answers — A or B, black or white, yes or no — denying them the more nuanced view that the world is ambiguous and free form and contains many possibilities.

Obviously, as parents we all want to make sure that our children end up equipped to look after themselves, to be able to participate economically in our society, and to have meaningful and challenging work. The question is, what is the best way of doing that?

Some Tips for Career-Proofing Your Children

Promote self-knowledge: Instead of encouraging your children to prepare themselves for jobs, encourage them to know themselves and discover what they do well.

In what areas does your child excel? Do you give her feedback on those skills and abilities? Do you help her reflect on her experiences so that she can start the process of self-discovery? For example, does she prefer to study alone or in groups? Does she take feedback well? Does she have difficulty disciplining herself to do private work as opposed to projects with classmates? What has she learned about herself from the feedback of other people when working in groups?

Avoid the top-10 syndrome: As we've seen, it's all too easy to become seduced by the yearly predictions of soothsayers of what is going to be "hot" or "not" in the next decade. But too many factors, whether the Asian flu, new technology, changes in legislation, or new inventions around the globe, can render today's hot career choice quickly obsolete. Instead, you and your child should think about roles and areas of competence, rather than preparation for specific occupations. For example, is your child a social organizer at school, a natural leader, theatrical, a great presenter, critic, or devil's advocate?

Even if you could second-guess the market, it's unwise to encourage children to mold themselves to fit market needs or trends. Their skills, talents, and preferences – not just the marketplace – should drive their career choices.

This doesn't mean kids can't begin exploring their options and considering different occupations – this process can be an exercise for them in self-discovery. For example, a teenager drawn to filmmaking can begin by asking himself what he finds interesting about it as a career, and what kind of working environment he imagines it will be. Or consider Sam L. He writes extremely well and has a wonderful command of language. He also has strong graphic and design skills and a good sense of storylines. Instead of having him focus on a particular occupation, he should be encouraged to think about a number of different possibilities, including photojournalism, video-game design, film direction, and advertising.

Above all, encourage your children to *pursue their personal passions.* Although this may sound blissfully naive, it in fact makes good career-planning sense, for the most effective choices are based on strengths and interests. And in the future, finding work that meets and reflects personal values as well as economic needs will increasingly become a prime determinant of career choices.

Lighten up: Don't try to force your children into premature career choices. Doing so may close down options which they don't have enough information to understand when they are 14 or 17. As a career counselor, I have met a lot of people who thought they had it right early in life, who have only now discovered the negative consequences of those decisions.

But really there is no such thing as getting it right. It's simply a question of better or worse choices. In the final analysis, whether our children are happily on their way in the workplace at the age of 24 or whether it takes another five years for them to find work they like will not really make any difference, except in the cost of additional education. Although it may be unnerving when kids start out in psychology, then move to engineering, then decide that's not right either, you have to understand that it is very difficult for your child to know what it is like to work as a psychologist or an engineer. Even if children have received career counseling, they still haven't had any hands-on experience to reflect and react to.

Putting undue pressure on your kids makes them anxious and resentful. It doesn't get them there any faster.

Don't impose your boomer values and world view on your kids: Parents, in talking about their kids who have not been able to focus or commit to a particular field of study, will often say, "When I was their age I knew exactly what I wanted to do." But what was true then is not true now, and saying this does nothing but irritate. We have entered a free-form career world where young people face intense competition for work, often with a sense that the chances for finding well-paid, challenging, and meaningful work are slim. In other words, consider the possibility that your experience may no longer be relevant.

Be careful, the kids are listening: When returning your e-mails from home are you muttering under your breath, "My boss the jerk . . ."? Or at the end of the day, do you complain about the "idiots" you work with? Well, guess what, congratulations, for once your child is listening.

Many young people are ambivalent about work because of what their parents have said over the years. Parents who are frustrated, who feel they have been passed over for promotions, who never share their joys or satisfactions but only their day-to-day irritations, have a profound impact on their children's long-term beliefs and feelings about work.

Share the positives as well as the negatives. Discuss real issues: budgets, plans that have gone awry, projects that were changed midstream, or the interpersonal skills you employed to turn around a difficult situation.

Pursue education at the highest and broadest level: A recent poll found that Ontario residents believe the skills acquired through a college or apprenticeship program provide better future jobs preparation than a university degree. This takes a very limited view of the future, ignoring the incredible global, technical, demographic, and environmental complexities with which workers will be grappling. Children should strive for the best education that is financially feasible, to the highest possible level. An understanding and appreciation of history, literature, and all the traditional humanities prepares people for dealing with a complex world. Learning how to learn and learning how to think are going to be critical imperatives for the future.

Promote self-esteem and emotional resilience: Make sure your children have the emotional wherewithal to deal with the failures as well as the successes associated with work, and the emotional breadth to relate maturely to people of diverse backgrounds and positions. Model for your children the skills they will need to withstand the emotional disappointments, stresses, and pressures that go hand in hand with work.

Foster trade and service skills: When I was a teenager, I used to help my father in his business on Saturdays, selling bridal veils. I wasn't that interested in bridal veils, but I gained a lot from the experience. In the first place, I learned something about myself: that I liked to sell, and that I was good at it. I also picked up some valuable business skills that have served me well throughout my career. I learned how to establish contact with customers, how to negotiate and close a sale, how to deal with a lot of people at the same time, and how to understand people's needs and respond to them.

Early opportunity to gain such skills will serve your children well, whether they ultimately go into business for themselves, go to work for an organization, or – as will most likely be the case – move in and out of different types of employment relationships. In a "Me, Inc." future, we will be managing our own careers much like a business – and that means knowing your own worth, being able to sell yourself, being able to negotiate contracts, and managing customer, client, and employer relationships well.

There are many ways trade skills can be acquired, from the traditional staples like lemonade stands, newspaper routes, lawn mowing, and baby-sitting, to running garage sales, buying, selling, and trading baseball cards or comic books, to starting an actual business. One 15 year old, for example, turned his passion for model cars into a highly profitable business trading them on the Internet.

You can use your children's business experiences to promote the development of trade skills by sharing your own business expertise and encouraging them to be reflective about what they have been doing, what they have learned, and how they can do things differently and better in the future.

Prepare your children to be good citizens: Your children will not only be units of economic productivity, but also global citizens. Think of the kind of roles you would like your children to play in society and the skills they will need to be effective contributors – and not just as workers but as leaders, volunteers, and members of the community. Help them embrace the values they will be expressing in those roles.

part three

The New Manager

The New Employment
Contract Comes Home to Roost

*P*icture this scene. It is an all-staff meeting. Management has just unveiled its business plan for the next 24 months. Significant change has been promised. But instead of getting the excited response from their staff they had anticipated, this is what they hear.

"You've told us this is going to unleash our creativity and enable us to stay closer to the customer and provide more value to them," one employee says. "But all I'm hearing is that I'll have even less resources for my job, and will have to work even longer and harder in this new super-lean organization. So, if I'm going to be giving you all this effort, and at the same time take responsibility for continuing learning, what I don't understand is what are you going to give me back? I can see what is in it for *you*. But what's in it for *me*?"

This question pinpoints some of the underlying tensions and difficulties with the new employment contract, a point I usually illustrate in my speeches with a pair of overhead slides.

The first slide shows how the organization defines the new contract: *"You are responsible for your own employability. We will provide you with meaningful, challenging, and skill-building work that will be good for your résumé, so long as you continue to add value."*

People nod. They have all heard the litany, ad nauseam. It has, after all, become the new corporate mantra.

The other slide shows what people really hear when organizations recite their mantras: *"We offer no job security. We will fire you when we have no more need for you. We will work you to the bone. We don't pay particularly well. And we will tell you that you are our most important resource."*

This second slide is greeted by the rueful laughter of recognition by everyone, including senior managers – in particular, senior managers.

Under the new employment contract, there is no loyalty between individual and organization; no commitment beyond the short term; no history beyond yesterday's results. Considered as a contract, it is extraordinarily one-sided. The organization gets the flexibility to hire and fire at will, without obligation and without guilt. Individuals get only vague promises of continuing growth and development, so long as they demonstrate their continuing usefulness. As one friend put it, "They call that a contract? I mean, would you sign it?"

In the days of the buyers' employment market, organizations didn't need to worry what their people thought. They could rely on economic insecurity and fears about job loss to keep people in line. Turnover was not a concern. Indeed, retention of staff was more often seen as a problem rather than a goal.

Talent Wars

There are signs, however, that the pendulum is beginning to swing back. Organizations describe talent wars as they compete for staff. The job market for managers and professionals has improved, particularly for in-demand knowledge workers in the systems area and in professional-service firms such as accounting, advertising, and consulting. Emboldened by growing demand for their skills, the very people whom organizations "empowered" to manage their own careers have become cocky enough to do exactly that. After all, being empowered means always being on the lookout to ensure that you are doing work that meets your needs, contributes to your employability, and adds to your résumé. So suddenly, for the first time in years, organizations are worrying about turnover and retention.

Turnover always increases in an improving job market. What is apparent today, though, is the apparent absence of any trace of loyalty on the part of staff to their current organizations. The chickens, as they say, are coming home to roost. Or as one job-hopper put it, "How can organizations expect us to remain loyal, given the shabby treatment we've received over the past few years?" Paradoxically, despite managers' lament of the loss of loyalty, that quality may still exist more strongly than they believe. For example, in a survey of 2,020 American employees, the Loyalty Institute found that approximately 66% intend to stay with their current company for the next several years and 50% would stay, even if they were offered a similar job with slightly higher pay elsewhere (*Canadian HR Reporter*, April 20, 1998).

There's no doubt that some organizations have handled their restructurings and downsizings of recent years clumsily, even downright callously. But even in the most humane and well-managed organizations, turnover is on the increase. And that's only to be expected: it's the flipside of the new employment contract.

Like it or not, we are all free agents now. Whether we work as freelancers, on contract, or as "permanent" staff, we are ultimately disposable when our services are no longer required. But by the same token, we can — and will — choose to move on to work that looks more rewarding or challenging. That is now the way of the world. And no matter how much individuals or organizations may want to turn the clock back to the old way of doing things, that simply isn't going to happen.

Rethinking Turnover

In this new atmosphere, organizations need to think what turnover means and whether it really is a problem. People move on for a variety of reasons. Some are reacting to a bad situation, such as a poor match with their skills, lack of future career prospects, or lack of opportunities for personal growth. Others are moving because they think – often unrealistically – that the grass is greener elsewhere. They believe that other people in other organizations are working fewer hours, have more resources, get more recognition, and are better rewarded. By providing staff with career-planning assistance, organizations can help people understand their own work situation better and realistically appraise their opportunities elsewhere.

But there will always be some people who, no matter how much they may like their current work, still want to go elsewhere to acquire new skills or be stretched in new ways. There is very little that organizations can do about this. Nor is it necessarily a bad thing.

I like to compare this to moving house. Sometimes you move because the house is falling apart or the neighborhood is going downhill – in other words, unpleasant things have happened since you've moved in. But sometimes you move because your needs have changed. It doesn't mean that there is anything wrong with the house or community. Rather, there is something out there that better meets your changing needs.

Organizations should certainly monitor the reasons for turnover to make sure that it doesn't reflect any internal problems. But insofar as there is no identifiable indication that such problems exist, then there's no reason to panic about people exiting the organization. Indeed, it could be argued that an organization that sees turnover as a *healthy byproduct* of empowerment has been effective in implementing the new employment contract.

Organizations may well bemoan investing time and resources to train and develop people who then move to another organization. But what goes around comes around. Often these organizations will themselves benefit from hiring people who have been developed elsewhere – who may represent a better match than the people they lose to turnover. In the long run, the result is greater flexibility for individuals and organizations.

A more mobile society, by extension, means more rapid and more frequent movement between jobs. Higher turnover was always a predictable outcome under the new employment contract. It's just that organizations are only now beginning to read the fine print.

Ten Strategies for
Managing the New Worker

I asked the senior-management team, "What do you want first, the good news or the bad news?"

Some years ago this organization had recognized that the nature of work performed by their front-line, mostly 20-something staff had changed significantly. Before, they were essentially expected to follow procedures and clearly defined policies. Now they were expected to be independent problem-solvers, capable of responding to a wide range of scenarios, acting as if they owned the business. The organization had gone out to hire individuals who filled this bill. Now they were struggling with the consequences.

"The good news," I told the senior managers, "is that you have risen effectively to the challenge of hiring the kind of front-line staff you want: people who are autonomous, who can take initiative, and who are independent problem-solvers. The bad news is that you have hired people who are autonomous, who can take initiative, and who are independent problem-solvers!"

The problem was that although they were hiring the right people, they couldn't seem to keep them. Morale and motivation were poor, turnover undesirably high. Management blamed this on a lack of loyalty.

Organizations often complain about the end of loyalty. But "loyalty" is a catchall word for describing a broad range of behaviors. It's true that in recent years we've seen the death of the unswerving identification of the individual to that abstract entity, the organization, that characterized old-style corporatism. But there still exists strong commitment on the part of individuals to their work. And after all, when managers say they want loyalty, what they really mean is they want people who display a high level of task dedication. The underlying motivation of such employees for this intense work commitment — whether to meet their own personal growth needs, advance their careers, or show commitment to the team — doesn't really matter.

"I was told that I was being hired to think outside the box. But every time I express an opinion, they look at me like I have some kind of contagious disease." This highlights some of the underlying tensions of the new workplace.

New workers, regardless of their individual psychological profiles, share a number of common characteristics:

- Concerns about employability. Workers today need to ensure that they have the skills to be capable of earning a living.
- A commitment to their work, team members, or profession over blind loyalty to their employing organization.
- A need to manage their complicated and harried lives.

Given the death of corporatism, forget the expensive company-logoed gift, unless it is a small token. There are several more successful ways to attract and retain good people, some of which have broad appeal and some which are more tailored to the individual.

I have already mentioned some of the different psychological profiles that dictate how individuals approach their work and careers. Some are independent thinkers or entrepreneurs, some are mainly motivated by lifestyle or personal growth, and some are careerists, authenticity seekers, or collegiality seekers.

Here are 10 general motivational and reward strategies that organizations can use to address some of the common concerns of the new worker, along with some specific strategies in response to the differing profiles of individual staff members.

1. Provide skill-building opportunities: Everyone can take a lesson from the 35-year-old manager who pitched a job applicant by writing down the three new skills she would be able to put on her résumé after she had completed her first project. All work can be potentially skill building, but it is up to the employer to articulate what the learning will be and how it can be useful to the individual. It's also important to remember that a skill-building opportunity is valuable to the extent that individuals perceive the skills to be meaningful to them in terms of their own career interests.

Skills can be acquired in a number of different ways, even in apparently dead-end jobs. Managers can encourage the process by matching workers with people they can learn from, giving workers opportunities to participate in cross-departmental task forces, setting up opportunities for them to shadow other workers in other jobs, and promoting cross-functional training. Some managers believe that their people can best acquire new skills by being thrust into situations that stretch them beyond their comfort level. Such managers are to be commended, so long as they provide a safety net.

2. Offer a personal pot of money: One life-insurance company, which takes its learning organization credo seriously, gives all staff a percentage of their salary to use for developmental purposes, whether for courses, travel to conferences, or books. Staff do not have to justify or explain their expenditures. Moreover, there are no expectations that the investment will pay off immediately on the job. Long-term career interests and ensuring one's ongoing employability are equally valid.

The sum of money does not need to be large, and managers don't need to prescribe how it is spent. One hotel chain with resorts staffed by many 20-somethings recognized the different needs of its staff by providing a small sum of money as a reward. The money could be applied to course tuition, spa services in their hotel, or ski lessons – you name it.

3. Use sabbaticals: With so many people today working to the point of exhaustion, smart organizations will encourage staff to take sabbaticals whether to recharge themselves, reflect on their next steps if they have come to a career crossroads, pursue a personal passion such as hiking in the Himalayas, or to finish a university program. A sabbatical as short as two months can be beneficial, though some people may need up to a year to truly recharge.

Sabbaticals shouldn't be tied to levels of hierarchy in an organization or length of service. Rather, they should be used to recognize that in the new work landscape people will have an ongoing need to retool. This means that weary baby boomers grappling with mid-life crises and 20- and 30-somethings seeking time off to travel or to test themselves in new ways are equally likely to welcome this sojourn from their everyday lives. Given the cost of replacing talent, this is a highly effective strategy for keeping people who may otherwise have jumped ship.

Interestingly enough, many people who take sabbaticals don't want to protect their jobs after their sabbaticals out of insecurity over their income. Rather, they really like their organization and want to ensure they can come back later. However, if they had not been given the sabbatical they would have quit.

4. *Provide career planning:* This is one of the interventions most frequently requested by staff and one that has a significant benefit both to the individual and the organization. The organization concretely demonstrates its commitment to individuals' employability. Individuals, meanwhile, typically discover that they like their work more than they thought and their company is not so bad after all. People establish goals based on their own interests, values, and strengths so that learning and developmental planning are tied to their personal needs.

In simple terms, career planning allows organizations to honor their side of the new employment contract, ensuring that staff have the skills to manage their careers.

5. *Establish company alumni clubs:* Savvy organizations will want to maintain contact with their talent, even after it has walked out of the door. Instead of seeing it as a rejection of the corporate culture, they will treat former staff members as ombudsmen who can refer new talent or clients and, more importantly, as valuable members of a potential talent pool who already understand the culture and may return to the organization with new skills in hand. One client organization, for example, routinely sends out a newsletter to its alumni. Organizations can also set up Internet chat rooms open to current staff as well as alumni. Instead of treating the exit interview as the final goodbye, managers can use it to communicate, where appropriate, an attitude of "good luck and we hope to see you again."

6. *Build on personal relationships:* Rather than assuming people have strong emotions about year-end results, build on the rapport that people naturally develop with team members and managers. People are committed to people and tasks, not to profit-and-loss statements. It is extraordinary how often it is the small and often banal gestures that are the most meaningful. People will often say things like, "I'm not really happy but I'm not yet prepared to jump ship because my boss was really good to me when my mother was sick." Or, "This project really needs me and we're a really tight team."

7. Provide flexible benefits: The Toronto Stock Exchange recently sent each staff member a toy dinosaur to underscore the extinction of their old benefits package. The old packages were being replaced by tailored packages to appeal to the diverse needs of different employee groups. Today's complicated personal and family configurations mean that people differ in the kinds of benefits they need and want. Increasingly, organizations are providing employees with a menu of benefits they can choose from, no longer assuming that everyone has the same tolerance of risk and need for long-term protection. While a young family, for example, may want orthodontic coverage, older workers may prefer higher drug benefits.

Nor is everyone a member of a nuclear family. Almost a quarter of urban, educated women born between 1946 and 1964, for example, are childless. Today, the U.S. Bureau of Labor Statistics calculates that the single and the childless are the fastest-growing segment of the workforce, a trend that demographers predict will continue.

Many large U.S. corporations now give everyone "benefit accounts" from which one can pay for health insurance for children, college tuition, child care, even legal insurance. In a similar vein, Kodak has changed its post-partum leave to a personal leave that provides employees with extended unpaid time to use as they wish, whether it be to prepare for a marathon, take a spiritual trek, or spend time with an infant.

Given the highly mobile nature of today's workforce, long-term pension plans may not be as attractive as self-managed portable investment portfolios. Young workers, for instance, know they have to take responsibility for their finances both in the short term and for retirement. They do not believe that government pension programs will be around for them when they retire.

8. Provide opportunities for eavesdropping: In my first job my boss, a therapist, invited me to hang out in her office when she was on the phone. I listened in on her returned calls to patients and learned a lot about how to handle many of the more difficult situations that arise in a clinical practitioner's profession. Eavesdropping is one of the simplest and most powerful ways to help someone pick up new skills. It can be accomplished in a number of ways. You could invite a sales associate to accompany you on a client call to an important customer, or to sit in on important meetings with management or clients.

9. Promote mentoring: Careerists and skill builders particularly benefit from being provided the opportunity to be counseled in everything from their career development to how to solve tricky political problems. Organizations can establish formal programs where they match employees with mentors from within the company, or they can let people select mentors from a pool. Ideally, individuals should partner with one or more persons who can teach them the basics or act as sounding boards.

10. Allow for project ownership: Many employees, particularly those who are more entrepreneurial, want to have the same kind of experiences they might have if they were running their own businesses. They need to feel that they own their own work, with both the upsides and downsides. They are prepared to take risks, including putting some of their own income at risk in return for a greater stake in the profits. If you allow staff to own a project, you must trust in their capacity and avoid micromanagement. Be there to provide support when needed, but don't force yourself into the picture.

Twenty-somethings, disdainful of large hierarchically organized companies, will be particularly responsive to management with this philosophy: "We trust you, we will support you in your risk-taking even if you make a mistake, we will fast-forward you to the highest level of responsibility where you can have a direct impact on the business, and if you're not having fun then there is something wrong."

Recognizing Personal Needs

One way or another, the 10 strategies above boil down to *recognizing personal needs*. One would be hard-pressed today to find an organization that doesn't pay at least lip service to the importance of work-family balance. Unfortunately, lip service doesn't take you to your kid's mid-afternoon soccer game, get you to the dentist, let you take unexpected time off to attend an out-of-town friend's wedding, or let you check out retirement homes for your aging parents. To the extent that organizations do have work-life programs in place – and it often seems to me that the more they talk about their policies, the less they are actually used – they are largely built around responding to emergencies such as child or elder care issues. In fact, all of today's workers are saying that opportunities for work-life balance are critical factors in determining job satisfaction.

Responsive employers will create what I call life-friendly organizations – cultures that support all individuals in their needs for personal time, whether for nourishing themselves and recovering from deadline-driven lives or in order to attend to family matters. This means more than flexible work arrangements or on-site daycare. It means ensuring that people can complete their work to their level of satisfaction while not making significant sacrifices in their personal relationships or other things they care about. It also means avoiding the "politics of overwork." One 33-year-old accountant who left an employer that did have a much-touted work-life policy put it succinctly: "I was prepared to give this job 100% in a 40-hour work week that would leave me 100% for the rest of my life, but 40 hours was never enough. Why should this company get the best of me, and my family only the dregs?"

Tired, Tired, Tired

Organizations that continue to reward staff with "command performance" off-site golf games and evenings at the racetrack may well be accused of suffering from a serious lack of creativity, not to mention insensitivity to the very demanding lives of their employees. As one 40-year-old director of marketing said about a day of corporate golf, "I hate golf. I resent spending money on clothes I'll never wear. I really like the people I work with but that doesn't mean I want to hang out with them, nor do I think we will be a more effective team because we shared some intimate expletives around a ball."

Organizations need to redesign their reward strategies to recognize the diverse needs of the new worker as well as each individual's unique values and interests so that the rewards are meaningful gifts.

Old Worker
vs. New Worker

Then	Now
Commitment is to company	Commitment is to self or work
Loyalty is to company	Loyalty is to team or manager
Other-directed	Self-directed
Seeks direction	Solves problems independently
Takes direction	Self-managed
Pursues career	Pursues challenge
Seeks promotion	Seeks self-fulfillment
Takes continuous career path	Follows zigzag career path
Long-term focus	Short-term focus
Values job satisfaction	Values work-life balance

The Coaching
Boom

At a recent meeting of industry executives, I was struck by the presence of a new group of people. In addition to the usual assortment of employed and unemployed managers and professionals, about 25% of the participants introduced themselves as "personal coaches."

Suddenly, personal coaching has become the hottest management trend since reengineering. From coaches helping small-business owners become more effective, to organizations hiring coach-consultants to work with their executives, to motivational guru Tony Robbins coaching President Clinton, it seems that everyone is getting in on the act.

Of course, the need to receive advice and counsel is not new. People have always sought informal advice and counsel, whether from a manager, friend, mentor, parent, or priest or rabbi. What is new is the *professionalization* of personal coaching. (Witness the number of courses, schools, and professional designations devoted to coaching now sprouting up across North America.)

In part, these new professional coaches are simply filling a vacuum. Previously, people could routinely seek advice from their managers. Today that's not always possible. Many managers are simply too beleaguered themselves to spend much time coaching their staff. And where in less harried times one might have sought out a friend to use as a sounding board, today one worries about taking up that friend's precious time – assuming, that is, that you can coordinate your busy schedules to even sit down together once. Enter, therefore, the personal coach to pick up the slack.

In addition, the growing fragmentation of society means that traditional social networks – whether based in community, religion, or family – have broken down. Many people are feeling lost and unprotected. These feelings are exacerbated by the complexity of the times we live in. As people struggle with a free-form world in which all the old rules about life and work and how to get ahead are no longer true, the promise of professional coaching becomes more enticing. In a world where we feel increasingly anonymous, a coach is someone on *our* side, someone who takes our interests seriously, who will help us to be the best we can be.

In sports, coaching is what happens when things get *serious*. You don't see coaches in the school playground, where children play informal pickup games. You see them when play becomes competitive, from t-ball leagues and up. Similarly, the new popularity of coaching in business circles is a direct reflection of the toughness of the contemporary workplace. The bar is set so high these days, and the competition is so fierce, that people feel the need for a coach to pump them up to a higher level of performance.

Coaching vs. Counseling

In a recent meeting a manager went through verbal contortions to avoid using the word "counseling," saying that she had gone to see someone for "counseling . . . I mean, um, advice . . . I mean, coaching."

The fact is that coaching is a much easier sell in the business world than counseling. Seeing a counselor has significant clinical overtones, and may be viewed as a sign of weakness or neediness. (There is no room for wimps in this tough new work world.) But going for coaching with its connotation of hard-edged, skill-based improvement is much more socially acceptable.

Indeed, given the glamour of big-time professional sports these days, going for personal coaching is more than just acceptable. It's seen as admirable, even sexy. It shows you are taking your work seriously indeed and making yourself as effective as possible as part of your ongoing improvement plan.

Organizations, therefore, will often willingly pay for something labeled as coaching while hesitating to contribute to counseling, which is seen as "touchy-feely," "mucking about in people's heads," not oriented to the bottom line, and so on. Male managers, in particular, are more comfortable with the sports-based language of coaching, with its promise of measurable improvements in performance and productivity, kind of like a *personal trainer* for the boardroom.

I find this distinction between coaching and counseling somewhat disturbing in that it can lead to an extremely narrow way of thinking about coaching. People go to coaches for a variety of reasons. In some cases, they are simply looking for some tips they can apply right away to improve their presentation skills, their dress and deportment, or their boardroom polish. The support they want is tactical and after one to three short sessions, they feel their needs have been met.

But there are also those who seek coaching for deeper life and career issues. They are working so hard, they feel that they have somehow lost sight of what's really important in their lives. They are asking whether their work is really meeting their needs. Or they may be feeling that something is missing in their lives. Sometimes they are experiencing a profound sense of emptiness: they have achieved everything they set out to achieve . . . and now what?

Then again, perhaps they have experienced a personal crisis, such as the death of a parent, the end of a relationship, sending children off to university.

In other words, there are many situations in which people are seeking much more than instrumental advice on how to improve their performance, catch the eye of the boss, or get that promotion.

Characteristics of a Good Coach

John D. is very proud of his coaching skills. He boasts about his success rate in turning around two troubled companies and his understanding of the new market forces. He feels particularly qualified to coach CEOs and senior vice-presidents because he's "been there."

I watched John try to sell himself as a coach to a senior manager wrestling with the fallout of a merger – significant layoffs. What John failed to understand was that the manager wasn't asking for help with a business decision – that part he had taken care of – but for help with dealing with his emotions about having to let so many people go.

In addition to understanding the business environment, good coaches will also be *capable counselors*. They will show many, or all, of the following characteristics:

- A holistic approach to the individual.
- An ability to tailor the intervention to the needs of the client.
- Knowledge of when to back off and when to push.
- Sensitivity to individual differences.
- An understanding of the new work landscape.
- A genuine desire to help.

Let's look at each in turn.

A holistic approach to the individual: A good coach works with individuals to increase their effectiveness in *all* areas of their life, both personal and professional. That involves helping them identify how they want to live, how they can achieve what they want from life, and what might be getting in the way of their being who they want to be.

By this definition, many of today's self-styled personal coaches like John D. fall short. Indeed, many have no real qualifications to fill the role. Often they are former managers with impressive management and leadership experience and a solid understanding of business issues. This may equip them to coach on pragmatic issues, such as working with people on their leadership styles or thinking through long-term business strategies. But these presenting issues often mask deeper underlying conflicts interfering with people's effectiveness, such as questions of personal fulfillment, authenticity, and fit.

David P., a 45-year-old executive, was having problems as a team leader, and the morale of his staff was suffering. He was sent for coaching. But what was supposed to be a relatively straightforward intervention to improve his leadership skills turned into something more complicated. The coach found that David was suffering from a profound career malaise, which was spilling into his work environment. Basically, David was having a values crisis and was unsure that he wanted to spend the next chapter of his life "producing more widgets." It was this *values crisis*, rather than weaknesses in his leadership style, that needed addressing.

An ability to tailor the intervention to the needs of the client: A good coach recognizes and appreciates the unique strengths and goals of the persons they are counseling. Rather than using a "one-size-fits-all" approach, they tailor their intervention to reflect what would best meet the needs of their clients. At their best, they see hidden strengths and can recognize, describe, and articulate those strengths.

For one woman, this was almost an epiphany. "I always thought I wasn't good at presenting in groups because I would get so nervous," she said. "But my coach saw my nervous energy in a different way. He said it was like a magnet in drawing and holding an audience's attention. So now, rather than avoiding giving presentations and trying to repress my nervousness, I've learned to cultivate it and use it as an asset."

Knowledge of when to back off and when to push: A good coach knows when to withdraw: they recognize that they have no more to offer their clients, or they realize that their own vision of what the clients can be does not match the clients' own goals. In some cases, they may recommend someone else who they feel will do a better job. Clearly this is a very difficult and challenging call, requiring a *sensitivity to individual differences*. Unfortunately, it is one that many self-styled coaches are quite unable to make.

Sensitivity to individual differences: A good coach will often want to stretch you beyond your comfort level. Sometimes, though, a coach will be so convinced about what her client is capable of achieving, that she may not be able to hear what her client actually *wants* to achieve. Either the coaches don't see the same barriers and obstacles that the client sees, or else they discount them.

For example, Carol C., a marketing manager, had always flirted with the idea of self-employment and was increasingly feeling that she did not fit corporate life. On the other hand, as a single parent, she had genuine needs for some kind of financial stability and income predictability. Carol's coach was so convinced of her ability to make it on her own that she dismissed her financial concerns. This was in part because the coach had never valued financial security herself.

A coach is sensitive to these underlying issues and understands concepts of individual differences, adult development, and career and life stages, as well as the complex interpersonal dynamics of business relationships. (Many have a background in psychology or other behavioral sciences and therefore have a good grounding in personality theory.) This sensitivity should be accompanied by the cognitive capabilities and business skills to see and understand the big picture.

An understanding of the new work landscape: A good coach understands the new work landscape, whether it be the frenzied schedules of workers, their struggle to balance work and personal life, or the new complexities of how work gets done. If coaches are from a different generation than their clients, they should be sensitive to realities of that generation, rather than imposing ideas and concepts based on old expectations or what used to be true.

A genuine desire to help: When you ask coaches why they like coaching, they often mention having the opportunity to "make a difference in someone else's life," "contribute to someone's development," or "give something back to the people."

Perhaps most important of all, then, a good coach is also someone who has a *genuine* desire to play a role in supporting and facilitating the development of other human beings. Unfortunately, many of the coaches I've met define their own success in terms of the status of their clients.

One woman in describing her coaching business talked at length about the CEOs she has coached, and then indicated at the end of her presentation that she could occasionally fit people with less lofty positions into her consulting practice. The subtext, essentially, was "I must be an important person, because I work with CEOs." For such people, the motivation to coach is tied up with a need to confirm their own self-worth, along with a desire to be close to senior management and feel themselves to be on the inside, and "in the know."

How a Coach Can Help

How can a coach help you? Often, people think they need to be coached in identified areas of weakness. For example, a small-business owner with no aptitude for marketing wants to learn how to market, or a middle manager wants to develop skills in networking. With concerted effort, it is possible to develop skills in areas where you have difficulty.

However, unless improvement in specified areas of weakness is *critical* to your work, you are usually better advised to focus on what you already do well. Spend your time developing further skills in those areas, rather than focusing on areas where you have no underlying aptitude. Typically, you will get more return for your investment of time and effort. Ask yourself what the cost would be of *not* improving yourself in those areas. How likely are you to be successful in your efforts? What will the cost of those efforts be in terms of time and money? Are there other areas you could be focusing on that will give you a greater return on your development investment?

At the same time, if you are entering a coaching relationship consider this an opportunity to examine your life, both professional and personal, at the broadest level. Instead of limiting yourself to enhancing one skill so that you will be more effective in your work, be prepared to take a journey to unexpected places. The results may be both surprising and rewarding.

The Manager
as Career Coach

*D*ave L., a 40-something administrator, has always been a good performer. But lately his work has deteriorated and he often seems cranky and irritable, sometimes getting into conflict with other team members. The reason: David is exhausted due to a combination of work and family pressures. Following reengineering, he is working much longer hours while also grappling with the problem of organizing living arrangements for an aging parent in another city. Dave has asked his manager for a meeting to discuss modifying his workload.

Sharon C., a high-performing sales representative, is unhappy due to a restructuring of her work. Where she was once relatively autonomous and able to act on her own initiative, Sharon's job now involves much more teamwork and consensus decision-making, a process she finds tedious and irritating. She is planning to ask her manager for a move.

Who Are You Going to Call?

Where do people who work for organizations turn first for career advice?

Usually to their managers. Like it or not — and many managers clearly don't like it — it has become part of the manager's role to act as a kind of career counselor. And this is particularly true in today's fast-shifting economy.

These are challenging times for managers, who have to maintain the morale and productivity of the people reporting to them even though insecurity about the future is rampant; traditional rewards for performance, such as promotion or salary increases, may be limited or unavailable; and individuals are facing extreme pressures both at work and in their personal lives.

To support the people reporting to them, managers must become involved in a broad range of work and career issues, in some cases going well beyond the traditional management role. They need to be attuned to the complexities of people's lives — to their anxieties about financial pressures, concerns about balancing work and personal life, and worries about future job security.

Making this situation all the more challenging is the fact that the manager may be grappling with some of these same issues themselves. They, too, may be feeling over-stretched and underappreciated. They can understand what members of their staff are going through, but may feel overwhelmed by the demand for personal attention just when they themselves are feeling overwhelmed by their work.

From the individual's point of view, seeking career advice from their managers makes good sense. The manager, after all, is in the best position to observe their work at first hand, offer feedback on their skills and potential, and help match up their aspirations with current and future organizational requirements. Moreover, where appropriate, the manager can refer individuals to other sources of information and can advance their plans at higher levels in the organization.

When managers hold regular career discussions with staff there are significant benefits for the individual, the manager, and the organization as a whole.

The individual gains better understanding of the links between performance, organizational expectations, and career opportunities. The manager opens up new channels of communication with staff, has the opportunity to renew enthusiasm and motivation, and is given the opportunity to provide practical career support. The organization benefits, too, gaining new and better information on the individual's skills, interests, and aspirations – information that can be put to good use in assessing training and development requirements, and in succession planning.

And yet despite these potential benefits, managers are often ill-prepared to take on a career-counseling role. Many are extremely uncomfortable with the whole idea.

Why Managers Can't Coach

Why do so many managers dislike acting as a career counselor to staff? Usually because they see this role as onerous. They see it, in fact, as much more burdensome than it really is – or at least, much more burdensome than it ought to be.

Counseling staff on career issues can be a relatively straightforward, even enjoyable, process – if organizations provide managers with appropriate support for their efforts.

Let's examine some of the most common objections raised by managers to counseling staff:

"I'm not a therapist." Many managers have found career counseling to be a painfully one-sided process. Typically, as they describe it, the individual presents a problem or concern ("I'm bored," "Where should I go next?", "What should I be good at?"). The individual then sits back, expecting the manager to do all the hard work of drawing out their ideas, extracting and interpreting information about their skills and abilities, and matching all this up with career opportunities and work assignments.

A thankless task indeed. Small wonder that so many managers complain about having to "play therapist" and "mess about in people's heads." Such a one-sided exchange makes heavy demands on people who are not trained in this area. Indeed, it would be difficult enough even for people who are. Professional counselors, after all, don't usually *tell* their clients what to do. Instead, they provide structured frameworks to enable individuals to discover that for themselves.

Structure is precisely what is missing in the typical manager-employee career discussion. And usually it is the organization that has failed both parties − by failing to provide individuals with the necessary tools to hold up their end of the discussion.

Giving staff the tools to plan their careers − whether through workshops or self-study career-planning materials − makes them articulate about their career interests. Instead of offering empty platitudes ("I enjoy working with people"), they can spell out precisely what they are looking for to build their portfolios, and what they see as their key strengths and developmental needs.

What ensues is a dialogue based on mutual respect between two human beings rather than the more authoritarian doctor-patient model, where the patient describes the symptoms to an all-knowing professional who diagnoses the problem and prescribes the remedies.

Managers no longer have to perform a marathon to draw out individuals but can instead simply respond to their well-framed questions and concerns and offer realistic feedback on their strengths, weaknesses, and goals. (As one manager, whose organization recently provided staff with career-planning tools, commented: "It was great. I could just sit back and listen. It was the best career discussion I'd ever had, resulting in some very concrete developmental decisions.")

This doesn't mean that you abdicate all responsibility to provide support. In fact, your role is more pivotal than ever. The difference is that, working within a well-structured context, you are much better able to provide useful help.

"We don't have clear career paths." In the days when organizations could confidently construct elaborate career paths, career development was a matter of showing staff how to get from job A to job B to job C. Today, no organization can provide such precise career-pathing information. The world is changing too fast. It's hard enough to keep abreast of current changes in jobs and staffing requirements, let alone to make meaningful predictions about future needs.

That's why, increasingly, organizations are placing responsibility for career planning on the individual. Individuals, after all, are in the best position to assess their own skills and interests, and decide on future work and life options that are satisfying and personally meaningful.

Rather than showing people how to get from job A to job B, career planning should *educate* them as to who they really are and what they really do at work. Instead of narrowly focusing on their job titles, and preparing themselves for jobs that may not even exist, people should look at *what they do* at work. They should examine not only their current position and specific technical skills, but also the *broader context* of their work to understand how to achieve greater satisfaction. They should be looking at the "Five Ws" of career planning (these are covered in more detail in the Conclusion to this book):

- *Who* do I want to work with? And how much interaction do I require with my co-workers?
- *Why* do I work? What is the purpose of my job, and how does it fit into the bigger organizational picture? And how well does it mesh with my own values?
- *Where* should I work? What kind of work setting suits my own work style and allows me to perform most effectively?

- *What* skills do I want to use? Technical skills, such as computer programming, marketing, accounting – skills acquired through special training? Or more general skills – leadership, writing, oral presentations, team-building – that are readily transferable from environment to environment?
- *When*? Do I prefer a fast-paced work environment, where I handle many tasks simultaneously, or a slower, more deliberate pace?

When people say they are unhappy with a job, for example, they may be *confusing the technical aspects* of the job as representing all the elements of the job. Typically, it's not the technical aspects (the *what* of the job) that are bothering them, but one or more other aspects (the *who*, *why*, etc., of the job).

By examining all these elements, people can look beyond their current job titles to discover their real skills, values, and preferences. They can then identify the areas in which they are most likely to be able to contribute, so that they can make informed decisions and set realistic career and life goals.

"With so much change, how can we talk about career planning?"
Actually, the rapid pace of change makes career planning *more crucial than ever*. Unless we develop and pursue a vision, we will simply drift, buffeted by successive waves of change, never sure exactly where we're heading. By setting goals, we take control over the future.

Career planning today means thinking about the landscape of work and opportunities in a radically different way. It means keeping your skills portfolio updated so that you can make the most of opportunities for satisfying and meaningful work.

"We'll be asked questions about future jobs we don't know."
The further we look into the future, the more difficult it is to say what
opportunities will exist, or what skills and experience will be required to take
advantage of them. But we can still have a good sense of the general skills
and competencies people will need.

Given the rapid pace of change, it no longer makes sense to prepare for
jobs. We need to prepare for areas of competence, types of work, and roles.
Encourage your staff to look at their competencies in the light of probable
organizational needs, and to develop learning goals that support their future
employability – inside and outside the organization.

"Won't career planning raise expectations?" Sometimes managers
express concern that talking about career development will spark unrealistic
expectations of opportunities for advancement.

Most people *already* have expectations, realistic or not, about their
careers. Far from raising expectations, career planning helps people develop
a much better understanding of the realities of organizational life. It asks
them to match up their skills, interests, and goals with the opportunities that
are realistically available to them, taking into account both their own skills
and potential and the requirements of the organization. And where their
current goals prove to be unrealistic, it assists in identifying alternate routes
to career satisfaction.

"Everyone will want a career change." Occasionally, some managers
are reluctant to encourage staff to explore other functional areas, fearing that
they will be deluged with requests for transfers to other areas of the organization, or worse, staff will want to leave. Engineers will want to move into
marketing, marketing analysts will yearn to manage, and so on.

Of course, many people like to muse about the idea of career change.
They *think* they're unhappy in their current job, and they wonder if the grass

might not be greener elsewhere. But most people, once they go through the career-planning process, conclude that their current work, with perhaps some minor adjustments, is fundamentally a good match for them.

Sometimes people will want to make more use of certain strengths, or to develop skills required to attain future career goals. But these requirements can often be satisfied by enriching current work. Requests for dramatic changes, as opposed to shifts in emphasis, are the exception rather than the rule.

In any case, when an organization supports individual career self-management, it does not assume a responsibility to meet everyone's expressed desires. Its only responsibility is to provide the tools and mechanisms that will enable people to plan and manage their careers effectively.

"I'm over-stretched already." In today's leaner organizations, many managers are already feeling beleaguered. Whole layers have been cut out, both above and below them. Administrative support has been reduced. Prospects for their own advancement appear more limited than before. These managers, as a result, see themselves as working harder than ever for less rewards. And they feel doubly beleaguered when staff clamor for help with their careers.

This is, in fact, a very strong argument in favor of providing career-planning assistance to managers as well as to their staff. Once managers go through a career-planning process themselves, they feel more positive about their own careers and more enthusiastic about helping staff members.

At the same time, assuming that staff are provided with effective career-planning tools, the pressure on the manager is actually reduced. In my experience, most managers *are* genuinely concerned about their staff and would like to help them with their careers — if they only had the time and the skills. Giving individuals appropriate tools reduces the demands on the manager on both fronts.

Common Career Concerns

People come to their managers with a variety of questions and problems. In some cases, these concerns will be specific to the organization: apprehension about the future, for example, in the light of a merger or acquisition. Other questions will be more general. Managers need to understand the roots of these concerns in order to provide effective coaching assistance.

Let's examine some of the common career issues on which individuals consult their managers:

"I'm bored/dissatisfied." Gary W. is an excellent technical trainer. But lately he has become increasingly bored with his work. "I teach the same courses over and over again," he tells his boss. "I'd really like the chance to try some internal consulting." Because Gary is such a good trainer, his boss is reluctant to have the courses taught by someone else. But she knows that if she doesn't give Gary some new challenges, his performance may suffer, or he may start to look for work elsewhere.

Boredom and dissatisfaction are always warning signals. When they are ignored, performance will typically decline, or else the individual may quit and move elsewhere in search of new challenges. In some cases, the individual may be heading for a full-fledged burn-out, as discussed below.

Some staff members, like Gary W., have no difficulty articulating their feelings of boredom and dissatisfaction. Others need some help defining exactly what is bothering them.

As a career coach, you can point to some of the possibilities. For example, has the person's job changed to become a poor match with his personal work style and preferences? Has the job become less challenging, or has it perhaps become *too* challenging because of increasing volume of work? Does the person get enough opportunity for visibility to senior management – or would he or she actually prefer less exposure? Or is the problem just a nagging feeling that other people in other jobs seem to be having more fun?

You can suggest areas to look at. But the individual contributor is the person who can best define the problem. If he is unable to pinpoint the causes of his distress, discussion should be postponed until he has gone through a careful process of self-assessment.

Once contributors define the problem, you will have to consider what you can do to meet their needs. It is not your responsibility as a manager to provide work that is constantly exciting and stimulating. Certainly, you should be as responsive as possible to the individual's requirements. But it is up to the individual to frame those requirements, and to ensure that they are realistic within the context set by your business objectives and available resources.

Sometimes you will be unable to meet their needs. Perhaps you don't have the flexibility or the resources, or the request is simply unreasonable. But often you will be able to arrive at a compromise that gives more of what they want. Gary W.'s boss, for example arranged for him to spend one day a week working as an organizational consultant. The company retained his excellent training skills the rest of the time.

You should also be careful not to impose your own values on the individual. You may think, for example, that a person is bored or dissatisfied because you know that you would be if you were in the same position. But actually that person may still be perfectly happy.

"What should I be when I grow up?" Peter K. thinks he might want to specialize in his field. But then again, perhaps he would be happier and more successful as a manager. "I don't know," he tells his manager. "I just don't know. What do you think I should do?"

No matter how strongly an organization communicates the message that individuals are responsible for planning their own careers, there will always be some holdouts — people who expect their managers to decide for them. They will ask, in effect, "What should I be when I grow up?"

Don't get drawn in. Send them back to do their homework.

"I'm burnt-out." Sandra G. used to be a high performer. But these days she seems listless and depressed. "I used to look forward to coming to work. But lately I don't feel like I'm accomplishing anything to my own satisfaction. There's always some new project demanding my attention. I try to keep up with everything, but it's hopeless."

At one time or another, most of us will experience feelings of being burnt-out and devitalized. This is a particularly common form of distress today, given the pressures that people are dealing with on so many fronts. People like Sandra G. feel involved in a never-ending routine of too much work and not enough recognition. Over-stretched, but under-stimulated, they feel that they are not learning anything new and have nothing to look forward to.

The burnt-out individual often appears over-stressed and emotionally fatigued — "flaring up" at the smallest cue, or appearing withdrawn and apathetic. Often they will complain of "losing their edge." Performance typically will decline.

Burn-out can have a variety of causes. Sometimes, the cause of the stress may be partly or wholly personal (financial or marital difficulties, for example). But it may also be strongly work-related. The person may be overstretched by current workloads.

Encourage the individual to undertake a thorough self-assessment, paying particularly close attention to:

1. Pacing and volume of work.
2. Nature and amount of stress on the job. Can it be reduced, or is it a function of role ambiguities or conflicts?

In some cases, the solution will be to restructure staff members' current jobs. In others, it may be necessary to reassign them to a position that provides a better match with their work style and preferences. Those who are clearly in psychological difficulty might best be referred for professional counseling.

"How did I get from there to here?" Ed H. is manager for an airline company. He is rated as a good performer and seems happy in his job. But lately he often finds himself lying awake, wondering, "I'm from a family of lawyers. How did I end up working in the airline industry?" Looking back on his career, it all seems arbitrary, somehow. Did he make the right choices? Did he make any choices at all?

One very common form of distress today among managers and professionals is the sense that their career is somehow accidental, arbitrary. They feel that they just "fell into" their line of work, that they never chose to become what they have become.

However, as we've already seen, our career choices are rarely arbitrary or accidental. Most of us are doing work to which we are well matched. But when we're under pressure, it may not seem that way. As mentioned above, most people who go through the self-assessment process conclude that their work — with perhaps some adjustments — is fundamentally a good match.

"I'm stuck." When Douglas C. joined his firm as a purchasing manager five years ago, he looked above him and saw four management levels between him and the president. He saw plenty of room to grow and develop and advance in his career. Douglas is still in the same job. But as a result of reengineering and de-layering, there are now only two management levels between Douglas and the president, and, he says, "A lot of people with better qualifications than me are quadruple-parked on the few spots likely to open up." Douglas is tired of being stuck in the same job, and depressed at

the thought that he has nowhere else to go.

Everyone's career ultimately reaches a plateau: a point from which further advancement in an organization becomes unlikely. Today, due to both widespread restructuring and demographic realities — too many people chasing too few opportunities to advance — people like Douglas C. are often hitting a plateau at a relatively early stage in their careers. A career plateau may be either:

- *situational:* the individual still has potential to move up, but the organization has no place for them to go, or
- *personal:* the individual has achieved his or her full potential.

When individuals hit a plateau, there is always the danger that they will become demotivated and apathetic. As a result, they may well perform below their previous level. In some cases, too, they may become embittered, blaming the organization for their situation. Worse, they may "export" their bitterness to colleagues and subordinates, by bad-mouthing the organization to anyone who will listen. As a result, the morale and performance of their co-workers may suffer, too.

The starting point in managing plateaued individuals is the recognition that they can still make a contribution to the organization. Research shows that most people can adjust to the loss of upward career mobility. As a manager, it's your responsibility to ensure that they do. What they deeply resent is being treated as second-class citizens, unable to contribute in any significant way.

Work with plateaued individuals to find ways of keeping their jobs interesting and challenging. For example, you can provide them with:

- Job enrichment.
- Lateral moves.

- Opportunities to mentor younger staff members.
- The chance to work in cross-departmental task forces.
- Enrollment in meaningful and prestigious training programs.

These are all ways of saying that "we care about you, and we still value your skills."

At the same time, encourage the individual to develop new interests outside work to meet needs that cannot be met inside the organization, such as leadership in a charity or volunteer group.

"I'm worried I won't be able to cut it." Marjorie P., a bank teller, adapted successfully to the introduction of new technology. But she is having difficulty adjusting to the new emphasis on selling. Marjorie is a quiet, shy person who balks at the very idea. "Once it was enough just to process transactions efficiently," she said. "Now I'm expected to do that, and sell customers on new services. If I was any good at selling, I would have got a job in retail." Marjorie is making no effort to sell anyone anything.

Skills obsolescence happens when an individual's job has been changed dramatically, or made redundant, by new technology or market change. What can be done to salvage the situation?

Most people use a mixture of specialist and generalist skills in their work. When specialist skills become outdated, they may still have other, more generalized strengths to build on for the future. By going through a process of self-assessment, they can identify these strengths and investigate other work in which they can apply them. With the rapid pace of change, the threat of skills obsolescence is present in almost every industry. Encourage your people to:

- Anticipate and make plans for change; be flexible and adaptive in their thinking.

- Be aware of the downside of overspecialization.
- Build on transferable skills.
- Continue to update skills.

Marjorie's manager initially thought about sending her on a course in sales skills. But after Marjorie went through a searching self-assessment, it became clear that she would never be very happy or effective in a sales role. But she had some considerable strengths in other areas, including problem-solving and analyzing information. She opted to move into the Information Systems area, where she is both happy and productive.

"I've been in this job a year. When is my next move?" Some people, although they have not yet hit a plateau, are moving up much less rapidly than they would like. They are rated as having high potential. They have been told that the organization sees them as tomorrow's leaders – but for now, there is no room to promote them.

The risk is that these high achievers will jump to another organization in search of speedier advancement. Faced with that risk, managers may try to hold on to them with promises of advancement they cannot keep.

By making such promises, managers only undermine their credibility and store up trouble for the future. It's much better to confront the situation now. Managers should be honest and realistic with these impatient high achievers, encouraging them to develop a better understanding of their situation through career planning.

In some cases, as a result of such planning, the high achiever will decide to look for opportunities outside the organization. But almost certainly they would have done so anyway, sooner or later. And typically they will discover that most organizations are operating under the same constraints.

In the meantime, you should work with your high achievers to make their current positions as stimulating and challenging as possible. They will appreciate the opportunity to learn new skills that will be instrumental to their long-term career success. They are also extremely responsive to psychological rewards, such as status and prestige, or being given responsibility for a high-profile project with major visibility to senior management.

"I'm ready for promotion — don't you agree?" It's a common aggravation. A staff member believes it is time for an upward move, but as her manager you don't share that assessment. And no matter how bluntly you explain this, the individual continues to overrate her abilities and potential.

Almost immune to criticism, unable to distinguish between politeness and fulsome praise, such individuals might be thought of as "pronoids" (a term first coined by Queens College sociologist Fred H. Goldner). Where paranoids suffer from delusions of persecution, pronoids have delusions of admiration. They can be extremely exasperating people to have around.

Faced with a pronoid individual, some managers become quite infuriated ("How can I make him understand that he just isn't ready?"). But your responsibility here is only to give clear and honest feedback, not to persuade the individual of its accuracy. Some people will indeed choose not to hear what you are saying. But so long as the individual is doing his or her job well, it's really not worth getting upset about.

A Coach — Not a Fortuneteller

People look to their managers for assistance on a whole range of career-related issues. And managers can indeed provide valuable help — so long as the ground rules are clearly defined, and individuals are empowered to acquire the information they need to make informed and realistic career choices.

Managers are not psychiatrists or fortunetellers. But in a well-structured counseling situation, they can be highly effective coaches.

Mentors
Show the Way

*F*red and Ken W. graduated from the same MBA program in the same year and started their careers in similar jobs with similar companies. Five years later, Fred has done quite well and is a director of marketing. But Ken has done even better: he was recently appointed assistant vice-president.

When Fred and Ken compare notes, one key difference emerges. Ken has always had a mentor – someone who has taken an interest in his development, and has been a source of advice, guidance, and support in his career.

A mentor is someone who typically acts as a sounding board, coaching you in effective behaviors and providing insight into everything from how to handle a tricky situation, to how to pitch a client or get a bank loan, to how to deal with corporate politics. Sometimes he or she may also open doors for you and act as an advocate on your behalf.

Research shows that successful people almost always have had one or more mentors. The classic mentor-mentoree bond in these studies was an informal one. But by the late 1970s, with growing recognition of the importance of mentors in career development, organizations had begun to experiment with more formal mentoring programs. Today, interest in mentoring, whether formal or informal, is exploding. At the same time, the mentoring relationship itself is changing to reflect new pressures and new work realities.

There are a number of reasons why mentoring has become such a hot topic. In a quicksand economy where the old rules of career success no longer apply and productivity pressures demand that you get it right the first time, many people are looking for direction. And typically, their own managers, overwhelmed by their own productivity pressures and besieged with other demands, are unable to offer that support. Instead people look to a mentor for advice.

Organizations, too, have begun to take an interest in mentoring, in some cases sponsoring formal programs. This renewed interest goes well beyond a recognition of the positive impact that mentors can play in people's long-term career development. Organizations understand that their managers don't have the time to provide traditional career support for staff, and that mentors can help pick up some of the slack. Moreover, in organizations that have been largely denuded of wisdom by massive restructuring and downsizing, mentoring offers a mechanism for capturing and transmitting the embedded wisdom of the older staff who remain.

Mentoring programs have also been introduced in recognition of the fact that many people need "a leg up" and don't have access to informal mentoring assistance. In organizations, for example, informal mentoring relationships have always existed between male senior managers and high-potential young men – while women have had few such sources of informal support available to them. Providing women with formal mentors helps level the playing field.

Similarly, there are many groups – whether people starting their own businesses, young people entering the workforce, immigrants upgrading their skills – who are starting to benefit from mentoring initiatives.

The first step in a formal mentoring program is to identify potential mentors. Not everyone has the right psychological makeup. There are no hard and fast rules, but here are some key attributes:

- Ideal mentors derive a genuine pleasure from promoting others' interests.
- They are proud of the accomplishments of their protégés rather than threatened by them – even where the protégés go on to surpass them.
- They are adept at reading people and situations.
- They have an intuitive sense of what different types of work require in terms of personal characteristics, and where different work experiences can lead.
- They understand the business and can balance its needs against the needs of their protégés.
- They are sensitive to individual differences in personality and values.
- They welcome the opportunity to give something back, and to make a difference.
- Perhaps most important of all, they have a generosity of spirit.

Once potential mentors have been identified, some programs, almost like a dating service, match them up with mentorees. A potential difficulty with this approach is that if the match proves a poor one, the mentoree may be too embarrassed to change it.

It's important to recognize that mentoring is a *human* relationship with a strong emotional component. The mutual respect between mentor and mentoree can be facilitated, but it cannot be legislated. One approach that works well is to let mentorees pick from a pool of potential designated mentors (indicating their second and third choices as well, to help the organization ensure a balanced workload).

More Than Practical Guidance

Some programs legislate how often mentor and mentoree should meet, for how long, and what they should discuss. But while a framework can be helpful, don't look at the relationship mechanistically, or you risk stripping it of its vibrancy. Different people have different needs to talk to a mentor at different points in time. What they want to talk about will vary, too, depending on their age, personality, and their life and work situation. Carol, for example, may be looking at a career move into a high-profile project and seeks advice, while Peter is concerned about the balance between his work and personal life.

But while people differ in what they look for in a mentor, in general it seems clear that today they are looking for more than just practical guidance. Increasingly, they are looking for *broader emotional and psychological support* from someone who genuinely cares about them as human beings.

With the breaking of the traditional ties of loyalty between the individual and the organization, and the growing depersonalization of contemporary society, people are looking to mentors to act as their defenders and provide feelings of being nurtured. And in some cases – depending on the personality of the mentor – they may be expecting too much.

Jane C., for example, was deeply disturbed by an unpleasant work incident. She ran into her mentor's office and blurted out the problem, expecting her mentor to reassure her and intervene on her behalf, the way her mother might have done. But her mentor was preoccupied with something else and reacted coolly to the interruption, saying, "This is not the right time or place."

Other people expect a mentor to act as a kind of personal agent for them – not just guiding them but also promoting their interests and marketing them into new projects or positions within the organization. In fact, mentors do not necessarily do those things. Typically it would be rare to have a single mentor who would both offer career guidance *and* act as a marketing agent – although some people are fortunate enough to have multiple mentors who share these roles.

Finding a Mentor

If you don't have a mentor, you can find one. Look for someone either inside or outside your organization with a more developed career intelligence – someone from whom you can learn and who meets the criteria discussed above.

Your ideal mentor may be a previous manager; a manager in another area of the organization (giving you access to other areas); a client; an external consultant; a family friend; or someone you worked with on a project team.

In the past, a mentor typically was *older* than his or her protégé. In the classic mentoring relationship, a senior manager would take a younger high-potential version of himself under his wing and steer him into plum assignments. Today, though, this model is increasingly being turned on its head, with the changing composition of the workforce and the flattening of hierarchy. Today, an older worker may be able to benefit as much from mentoring by a young employee as vice versa. Where a younger worker may learn about "how things often get done around here," and who the key players are, from an older mentor, the older worker may benefit from having their traditional beliefs about work challenged by younger, more irreverent colleagues.

You may have more than one mentor. After all, given the multiple roles we play, many people are potential sources of support.

Traditionally, in finding a mentor, people thought about "chemistry." In fact, you may be better off with someone whose approach, style, and world view is dramatically different from yours. You can then take advantage of new ways of thinking about things.

The most important step in finding a mentor is determining how you can benefit from someone else's know-how and expertise. Start with a self-assessment. What are your relative areas of weakness given your longer-term interests? Who can help you develop in these areas?

One question people ask is, "How do I approach someone? For example, do I call them up and say, I'd like you to be my mentor?" The mentoring relationship need not be that formal. It can in fact be very fluid. For example, there are a number of younger women who call me for advice every now and then when they are wrestling with a problem. Consider approaching people whose opinions you value to ask them out for coffee. Tell them you'd like to pick their brain or use them as a sounding board.

Many people don't avail themselves of the help of a potential mentor because they worry that it's an imposition. Actually, having their opinions sought can be deeply satisfying to mentors. Far from feeling imposed on, they appreciate the recognition that they have some knowledge and wisdom to share.

How to Give
People a Belief in the Future

Ann Sanders, a vice-president with a large financial-services company, is a success by most people's standards. She has moved ahead rapidly in her career, while managing to maintain a strong family life. But lately, she feels close to the breaking point. "Most days I go into work early and stay late, but somehow I never catch up with the work. There's always some new priority, some new fire to fight. And every time I have to travel, the work piles up even higher. My boss is mad at me because I'm not delivering; my husband is mad because I'm always home late; and my kids are upset because they hardly see me. More and more I find myself thinking: Is it really worth it? If not for the money, I would quit tomorrow."

Mark Miller, a manager for a high technology company, is coping with the aftermath of a major downsizing. Forced to produce more work with fewer resources, he feels under siege. "Before I finish one project to my own satisfaction, I have to start on another," he says. "I'm not managing anymore, I'm just reacting to events. I really feel as if I'm losing my edge."

Linda Graves, a compensation specialist in an HR department that has shrunk from 12 people to 5, is being called upon to function in a generalist's role, juggling a broad range of issues. "I'm not happy in this new work, nor do I feel like I'm doing a good job," she says.

Jack Thompson was once a highly effective sales manager in a midsize manufacturing company, reporting to the vice-president of marketing. Following a corporate restructuring, Jack reports directly to the CEO and is being asked to play a more strategic marketing role. "I'm great at selling, but handling these more strategic issues just isn't my strength," Jack says. "More and more, I feel that I just can't do what they're asking me to do. It makes me start to question myself: Am I stupid? Incompetent? I never used to feel that way."

Fewer Rungs Left to Climb

Restructuring. Downsizing. Organizational change. As we have seen, these have become fixtures in the new landscape of work as companies scramble to meet the challenges of an increasingly competitive marketplace. Widespread elimination of jobs and reporting levels has created increased workloads for managers and professionals, while other jobs have changed to the point where they demand different competencies. And, always, there is the relentless pressure to produce.

Many people caught up in these sweeping changes are feeling beleaguered by the demands placed upon them now, and chronically anxious about the future. Often, they

- are working at such a frantic pace they are losing any sense of satisfaction or accomplishment in their work;
- are worried about the security of their income;
- no longer feel that they are making a meaningful contribution;
- have begun to doubt their own competence;

- are having increasing difficulty balancing work demands with their personal and family life.

At the same time, many people feel that the whole effort-reward equation has become unbalanced. Not only are they working harder than ever, they are often doing so for what they perceive as fewer rewards. Their career progress has slowed to a crawl. And when they look ahead they find it difficult to see where they can go. As reporting levels have been eliminated, there are fewer rungs left to climb on the traditional career ladder. And they know that jobs that exist now may not do so five years from now.

This sense of malaise is compounded when people are in the wrong job or work environment – something that happens all too often in the wake of restructuring and downsizing. Highly competent specialists like Linda Graves, in the example above, are turned into barely competent generalists. People with real strengths, like Jack Thompson, are shuffled into positions where their weaknesses come to the fore.

Perhaps the most pervasive stressor of all, however, is coping on a daily basis with the all-encompassing state of *ambiguity* that characterizes contemporary organizational life. People are plagued with such questions as:

- Will my organization restructure/downsize (again)?
- How will I be affected? Will I still have a job? What will it be?
- Who will I be reporting to?
- What will happen to the people reporting to me?
- Will this company/unit/division still exist a year from now?

Most people who work for organizations have been socialized to expect a much more orderly world – one in which the future is relatively predictable, and in which it is possible to engage in particular tasks to achieve particular outcomes. What we are seeing today is a pervasive anxiety, as people try to come to grips with a world in which the present is uncertain and the future almost completely unpredictable and uncontrollable. Faced with this chronic ambiguity, their whole sense of personal efficacy is being eroded.

Helping People Cope

People work to derive a variety of rewards: not only salary and the prospect of advancement, but also a sense of collegiality with co-workers; a feeling of purpose in their work; opportunities for development; identification with the goals of the organization; a sense that their activities are instrumental in contributing to producing desirable outcomes in the future. When these rewards are progressively stripped away, morale and performance will inevitably suffer.

The pressures on people in organizations are unlikely to abate for the foreseeable future. Instead we will likely see much more of the same. Jobs will continue to change or disappear entirely; companies will continue to sell off, or shut down, whole business areas; new technology will continue to transform how people do their work; market changes will require an ever-shifting mix of skills. There will be more restructuring, more downsizing – and even more pressure on the individuals caught up in these changes.

The challenge facing organizations is to help their people cope with these pressures by providing them with a *renewed sense of purpose.* People need to feel that they are making a real contribution in their jobs and that they are valuable both to themselves and to the organization.

What can organizations do to help their people cope, and restore their sense of the future? Here are five strategies:

1. Recognize that people are a nonrenewable resource. People today are juggling demands on many fronts: work, family, finances. They don't have endless resources for coping with the pressures placed upon them. Eventually they will be worn down, and their performance and productivity will decline. There is only so much you can ask of them.

2. Communicate clearly and honestly. Whether the issue is a downsizing, a potential merger or sell-off of assets, or simply the need to cut costs and improve productivity, organizations need to let their people know what is going on. When organizations keep their people in the dark, gossip and rumor will flourish – usually with a much more devastating impact on morale and productivity than the plain truth would have had.

The organization must paint a *compelling picture of the future* so that the staff will have a sense of how they can benefit from the coming changes. All too often, senior managers hide behind closed doors during a significant organizational change. When they come out, they walk about mournfully, looking like they just lost their best friend. They should recognize what they are actually communicating through such behavior, and fulfill their responsibility to deal openly and positively with staff.

3. Demonstrate an appreciation for individuals. Organizations can show that they care about their people in a variety of ways, ranging from simple gestures (like taking the trouble to say thank you for a job well done) to more complex interventions, such as the provision of opportunities for self-assessment and self-determination (see below).

4. Live up to the new employment contract. By now everyone knows that no organization can guarantee its people lifelong job security. But what organizations can and should do is ensure that their staff remain marketable, whether inside or outside the organization. And what that requires is supporting individuals in taking responsibility for managing their own careers. Loyalty can no longer be bought with promises of security – but it can be earned, by treating people with dignity and respect.

5. Provide opportunities for self-assessment and self-determina-tion. As well as encouraging people to take responsibility for managing their careers, organizations should provide them with the proper tools to do the job. People should have the opportunity to go through a meaningful process of self-assessment that enables them to plan out their goals. This can be provided in a number of ways, from the "Cadillac option" of executive coaching to career-planning workshops and one-on-one counseling.

How Effective Career-Management Programs Can Help

At first glance, this may seem to be a paradoxical suggestion. Why undertake a career-management program when, for most organizations and industries, so many question marks abound about future jobs or careers?

But it is precisely the uncertainty that makes career planning so vital. Career planning promotes morale and employability by:

- Fostering self-knowledge.
- Restoring a sense of self-efficacy.
- Communicating "we care."
- Preparing people for the future.
- Improving job fit.

Let's look at these benefits in detail:

Fostering self-knowledge: Career management helps staff move beyond identification with their existing jobs and job titles. Individuals no longer see themselves as filling a specific job (e.g., "I'm a marketing manager for ABC Company"). Instead, they recognize themselves as the *owner of a portfolio of skills and experiences* (e.g., "competencies and knowledge in marketing and sales; knowledge of financial products aimed at baby boomers;

team-building abilities"). They can then *reconfigure these skills* and experiences in new ways, either in the organization or outside it.

Restoring a sense of self-efficacy: Providing people buffeted by change with the opportunity for self-assessment can be extremely valuable in promoting individual and organizational renewal. The career-planning experience builds confidence and boosts self-esteem by reminding individuals of their accomplishments. It promotes an understanding of their marketability, both within and outside the organization.

Through self-assessment, people have the opportunity to sit back and reflect on how much they really *are* contributing now, if they only had the time to realize it. Reviewing their accomplishments gives people a renewed sense of self-efficacy in their work. As a result, their morale and commitment are renewed, too.

Communicating "we care": Supporting individuals in their career management shows them that management cares and is living up to its side of the new employment contract. The message is that people do have a future, whether it's inside the organization or outside.

Some senior managers might fear that introducing career planning in a period of uncertainty will only create panic by leading staff to believe they are about to lose their jobs. That's an old-fashioned concern, however. Today's workers aren't fools. They understand the challenges of the new employment contract and all but a few realize, at least intellectually, that they are responsible for managing their own careers. Implementing a career-planning initiative doesn't communicate they are about to lose their jobs. It communicates that the company wants them to be the strongest and most capable individuals they can be, and is willing to invest in them.

Some executives, of course, might harbor an opposite fear: that the initiative will only encourage their best staff to leave. In my experience, that fear is unfounded. If the organization is properly communicating with its staff, career planning won't encourage people to jump ship.

Indeed, the opposite has been the case. People come to career-planning workshops excited and appreciative that the company is finally doing something to support them in ensuring their employability, rather than simply paying lip service to the new employment contract. And even if at times they are nervous because their jobs are vulnerable, they come out feeling significantly more competent. Participants realize that they are much more employable than they thought, whether inside or outside the organization. People say, "I recognize that I'm marketable, and I'm comfortable waiting out this change, because this could represent an exciting opportunity."

Consider, also, whether you want individuals working for your organization who aren't highly employable elsewhere – and are clueless about their appeal?

Preparing people for the future: Self-assessment also assists people in preparing themselves to adapt to change in the future. It shows them how to look beyond their job titles to identify key underlying skills that can be transferred to other work settings. Once people gain a sense of their own "marketability," whether inside or outside the organization, they will be more confident in themselves and less anxious about the future.

Going through a career-planning experience typically assures staff that they have the strength to thrive in the future organization, whatever its shape – or that if they do lose their jobs, they have skills that can be used in other work. That makes them less defensive, more willing to accept change.

Improving "fit": It's crucial that organizations, as they change and evolve, ensure that people don't wind up in the wrong slots. By helping people understand their abilities and by boosting their confidence, career planning reduces the chance that individuals will grab at any opening just for the sake of continuing to hold a job with the company. Instead, they will understand what roles they are best geared to fit and which ones will further growth and advancement.

Take George, for example. A policy analyst at a large firm, he saw himself only as capable of continuing in that role after a merger. But through career planning, he realized that what had made his unit so successful was not its analytical research skills but the ability of people within it to build team relationships. When an opportunity presented itself that put a premium on team-building skills, he was comfortable in making the switch, thanks to his heightened self-awareness.

Self-assessment gives people who are currently in a job or work environment that represents a mismatch with their interests and skills the opportunity to identify the causes of their stress and do something about it. In some cases the solution will be some modification to their current work, to give them more of what suits them best. In other cases, a move – whether inside or outside the company – will be necessary to achieve a more satisfactory match.

Delivering Support

There are a number of vehicles for delivering career-management support for staff during periods of apprehension and change. The one I prefer is that which an organization would normally use for support in career self-management, whether it be a corporate university, leadership institute, management development program, or learning center.

I am less enthusiastic about some of the other vehicles. Making an Employee Assistance Program the sole mechanism to respond to staff apprehensions, for example, can send an implicit message that anyone having problems is not as emotionally strong as his or her colleagues. After all, an EAP is where you go when you are suffering from a personal problem. Obviously the EAP must continue to be promoted during this period. But HR should also be stressing more positive and less clinical approaches.

Career centers have also been used with varied success to help smooth transitions. When the career center is viewed as a vehicle for promoting employability and change, it has been successful. But when it is confined to delivering one-on-one counseling support, it can become like an EAP program, preoccupied with people who are *hurting*. That can become expensive and also result in the career center eventually losing touch with the many individuals it should be helping.

In other words, career planning should be positioned to help people:

- get started on the process of framing meaningful and realistic career and life goals;
- identify their unique work style and preferences profile;
- learn how to look beyond their job titles and identify key underlying skills and competencies that can be applied in future work assignments;
- identify the new skills they may need to develop to adapt to new corporate directions;
- make informed decisions about future job assignments;
- develop and implement personal career and life plans.

Making the Right Move

To see the potential impact of an effective career-management program, let's look briefly at the experience of a financial-services company. This company had already gone through a downsizing and was about to place one of its divisions up for sale. A company-wide meeting was called to brief people on the situation. Although no promises could be made about job security, management wanted people to understand that they recognized their apprehension and demoralization.

Subsequently, the company offered a series of career self-management workshops. The workshops were open to everyone, and over 80% of the employees opted to participate. Through these workshops, people were able to regain a sense of their own marketability. As a result, they were able to face an uncertain future with much greater confidence. The program had an obvious and direct impact on morale – including the receipt by senior management of dozens of unsolicited thank-you letters.

Giving Something Back

Obviously, organizations stand to gain some significant benefits from providing self-assessment and career-planning assistance to their people. Individuals become more flexible and adaptive. Morale and commitment are renewed.

Perhaps even more important, however, is the opportunity for organizations to show that they really do care about what their people are going through in these difficult times, and to demonstrate their concern by *giving something back*. And what they are giving back is nothing less than the individual's sense of well-being and personal efficacy.

part four

A New Set of Skills

Become a
Career Activist

*L*ately, I've been struck by the number of people who are unhappy in their work but unwilling, or unable, to do anything about it. They recite the usual millennial litany of being overworked and underappreciated, of managing their families at long distance, of "not having a life anymore." But for all their complaints that they aren't going anywhere, they also make statements like: "I'm just waiting for the package." Or, "Better the devil you know than the one you don't know." Or, "Maybe when X retires next year things will change."

The very language is revealing: fatalistic, unquestioning, resigned. At its extremes it reflects the helplessness associated with depression: "There's no point in trying to make a move. It's the same everywhere . . ." (Do you recognize yourself in this language?)

And then there are people who, poised to take advantage of a hot job market, *are* looking to move — with the number-one criteria being money, rather than what kind of life they want to lead or whether their work meets their underlying values. They say, in effect, "If I'm going to have to go to the wall for my work, I might as well get a whack of money for it."

Career Passivity

These are, in fact, two sides of the same coin. Both groups, in their own ways, are demonstrating career *passivity*. It's a paradox that in these days of empowerment and self-management many people who otherwise see themselves as independent, take-charge types demonstrate a kind of helplessness when it comes to how they spend their working lives. They act as if their work is an implacable force of nature, something they are powerless to change, and can only accept with resignation. Where once people complained angrily about their excessive workloads, now they seem only resigned to putting up with a kind of ongoing, low-level malaise.

Most of us understand that today we have to take an activist stance in relation to our health, our personal finances, or our children's education. We no longer trust in the goodness of others, or of institutions, to look after our interests. We act at the first sign of a problem in these other domains to protect our rights and try to control our own destiny.

And yet work – which plays such a critical role in determining how we feel about ourselves, how effective we are as parents, family members, and members of society – has become the last area for such personal activism. It's as if *we don't see ourselves as being worthy of protection.*

Ask people *why* they are working so hard and they typically don't have an answer. Routinely working 12 hours a day plus a day on the weekend has become their reality, and they no longer think about things being different. Probe further and you'll get passive responses like "you just get sucked in," "you know how it is," or "that's just the way things are these days."

This career passivity is not limited to overworked middle managers. Indeed, senior managers who see themselves as self-determining at work – making choices and redesigning their organizations at will – are just as likely to describe their work as though it were an immutable truth, saying matter-of-factly, "I can't go on vacation (or go to parent-teachers night or visit with friends) because I have work to do." Asked what the consequences of *not* working might be, they can't even entertain the thought.

In part, perhaps, we are just too tired, busy, and distracted to look after ourselves. But we are also, typically, ill-prepared to think like career activists and recognize that we *do* have control over many aspects of our careers, if only we choose to exercise it.

In contrast to people waiting for the package or moving jobs purely for money are those who are introspective, thoughtful, and activist in their attitudes to their work. As one woman observed, "I wouldn't allow myself to be abused in a relationship, so why would I put up with being abused in a job? When you're doing work for which you're not well-suited, or which doesn't make you feel good about yourself, over time it feels like abuse."

Career activism means *becoming an intelligent actor in your own life*: developing a thorough understanding of your current situation, and then taking steps to change it for the better. And that means first of all having a vision of oneself as *worthy* of meaningful work and a fulfilling personal life. You need to become vigilant on your own behalf in routinely scanning your environment to ensure that your work continues to meet your needs. Ask yourself:

- Am I engaged? Am I feeling stretched in a positive way?
- Am I learning, am I contributing to my employability?
- Do I feel I'm doing work that's important?
- Are my personal needs outside of work being met?

To be a successful career activist, you need to understand the external economic and social landscape, educating yourself about the new work and career realities and knowing what you need to do to ensure your continued marketability. But you also need to be attuned to your own internal, personal world: what engages you, what you care about, what gives your life meaning. Only by knowing yourself will you be able to make the right decisions about your career – decisions that reflect your most important personal values and concerns rather than the external measures of success such as salary.

You will then be able to think about yourself and your career differently, to rise above the frenetic busyness of everyday working life, to make choices in terms of your own agenda, to pursue your own goals. And you will learn to trust yourself – your own ideas, instincts, and perceptions.

People need to think about the long-term cost to themselves, not to mention their families, their workplace, and their society, of sacrificing that which gives their life meaning. Becoming a career activist is not a luxury. It's the key to a successful and rewarding career and life.

On Selling
Yourself

"If I'm good, my work should speak for itself. I shouldn't have to continually trumpet my accomplishments."

If you ask people, as I do frequently in speeches and workshops, to what extent they agree with this statement, the response is typically one of profound ambivalence.

Intellectually, at least, most people understand that one of the central themes of the new economy is the need to always look after one's own employability – which means, among other things, continually having to sell oneself. And yet many people, particularly managers and professionals of a certain age, feel that this sort of self-promotion is somehow unseemly and unprofessional, and that they really *shouldn't* need to do it.

We have all had to sell ourselves at one time or another, whether in interviewing for a job or selling the services of our business to a client. But in today's tenuous, shape-shifting workplace, we need to sell ourselves *hard* all the time. People who work for large organizations now find themselves in the same position as consultants and other freelancers, constantly having to gather testimonials, document their achievements, and pitch new work.

It is no longer enough just to perform well. You must also manage other people's impressions of how well you are performing. Like it or not, the only way to secure your employability is to turn yourself into a valued commodity, constantly selling yourself so that others will buy your services.

Many people *don't* like it. Reducing themselves to a package of assets and selling features ("I'm a customer-responsive, client-centered, profit-driven, value-adding, flexible, results-oriented team player . . .") leaves them feeling somehow less human.

There is also an interesting paradox at work here. In today's teamwork-sensitive environment, where the emphasis is very much on *we* rather than *I*, some people are extremely uneasy about drawing the line between what *I* did and what *we* did in order to claim credit for their individual contributions.

Often, too, people are at a loss as to *how* to go about selling themselves. They are unsure where to draw the line between simply drawing attention to their attributes and accomplishments and being obnoxiously self-promoting. And they wonder what the proper mechanics are for doing so: should they waylay people in the hall, take them out for lunch, or what?

I should note that there is a strong *generational difference* in attitudes to self-promotion. At a recent workshop at a bank I probed those feelings by asking participants to choose which of two statements more accurately described them:

- "I understand why I have to keep people informed of my accomplishments, but, to be perfectly honest, I feel very uncomfortable constantly promoting myself. After all, if I'm really good other people should know."
- "I feel comfortable letting people know about my accomplishments. After all, if I don't, how are they going to know?"

There was almost a perfect generational divide between these alternatives. Participants who were in their 20s and early 30s found the second statement reflected them perfectly. They were comfortable marketing themselves. They had entered the workplace at a time when opportunities were scarce and when the old employment contract was under siege. They understood, or at least learned very quickly, that the only way they could secure work was by aggressively selling themselves. They had no expectation that some benevolent employer would look after them and their career.

But almost to a person, those in their late 30s and 40s picked the first option – they simply weren't at ease in the self-marketing role, even though intellectually they understand the need for self-promotion.

A typical comment from that older group is, "I'm 45 years old – I shouldn't still be *proving* my competence."

Still, as one 20-something observed, while the 40-somethings may have difficulty in selling themselves, they, at least for the most part, have some place in which to do so. She and her friends, she said, had absolutely no problem marketing themselves – if only they could find a potential purchaser.

Suggestions for Reluctant Self-Marketers

Reappraise what it means to talk about your skills and accomplishments: Many people are self-conscious about talking about themselves, fearing that they will be seen as shamelessly self-promoting. Get over this self-consciousness – think of yourself as communicating useful information about how you can contribute to people who might be interested to hear about it. If you don't tell them what you are capable of, they may never find out.

Recognize that what is obvious to you may not be obvious to others: Don't assume that because you have told people something once, they will necessarily remember it. A friend was upset because she was passed over for a role on a high-profile project. "They knew I was the best person for the assignment," she complained. Six months before, when the project was first discussed, she had made a strong pitch for her inclusion, based on her skills and experience. I often hear stories like this one, and usually the problem is that "they" *don't* know or don't remember. People are so busy these days, and so buried in information, that they won't necessarily remember something you told them months ago. It's incumbent on you to remind them at appropriate intervals.

Avoid the "ego-dump": There's nothing I find more suffocating and off-putting than having to listen to someone recite a self-congratulatory litany of commendations, client bookings, sales results, or whatever else. Marketing yourself is no different from marketing any other product. *Edit your information* for your market. Focus on what they want and need to know about you. Make sure what you say interests *them* – not just *you.*

Remember the other person's ego: If you go too far in touting your own accomplishments, you run the risk of making the other person feel insignificant. He may feel his only value to you is as a repository for your achievements, or may compare himself with you and feel inadequate. You are providing potential purchasers of your skills information about what you can do. You should not be seeking affirmation or validation from them about your value as a human being.

Track your strengths and accomplishments: To do an effective job of marketing yourself, you need to identify your key strengths and accomplishments. Don't expect your boss or your client to do it for you. In today's often-thankless work world, they may well be too busy to notice what you're doing, much less give you meaningful feedback. Going through a careful self-assessment will help you determine what you have to sell, as well as giving you the confidence to point out your strengths to others.

Properly done, self-marketing can be an enormous boost to your career. It also can become, in time, second nature. The key is to be yourself. Avoid being overbearing, obnoxious, or mindlessly repetitive. But at the same time, don't fall into the trap of being so complacent that your golden deeds remain buried treasures.

The Right and
Wrong Ways to Network

*T*he fall seems to be a time of year when many people approach their careers with renewed seriousness. Perhaps they've done some stock-taking at the cottage and have returned to work determined to get back into high gear. Or perhaps they've come back to find the same problems they placed on hold for the summer: the job is still a poor match with their skills, the boss is still a jerk, another reorganization is coming down the pike.

Whatever the reason, every fall I get a flurry of "networking" calls from people looking for advice, information, and contacts. Typically they are thinking seriously about changing jobs, or going out on their own as a consultant, or changing their business strategy.

Networking is an increasingly important career skill. We all need to be plugged into a variety of networks to keep up with developments in our field and position ourselves to take advantage of new opportunities – particularly in today's fluid workplace, with its growing emphasis on short-term assignments and multidisciplinary project teams. And yet many people are very clumsy, if not misguided, in their networking efforts.

We all know people who are so highly *instrumental* in their networking that they completely turn us off. When Gary T. calls me, as he does every year or so, I know he's either lost his job, or is looking for some other type of help. In between these calls, I may as well not exist – and Gary's hearty congeniality when he does call does not conceal the fact that this is clearly a fair-weather friendship.

Other people, however, are so uncomfortable about the whole idea of networking that they do it as little as possible. They think of it as being manipulative and exploitative – *using* other people to help them get ahead. Or they feel it is somehow *unseemly* for them to have to schmooze or glad-hand. They see networking as fundamentally insincere – feigning interest in people when all you really want is to use them for your own ends.

Rather than being about using people, networking is really about expanding your relationships and developing *mutually supportive relationships*. It is as much about being there for someone else as about using someone else to get ahead. When you network properly, the other person is as likely to be the beneficiary as you are. You might learn about a possible merger at a customer's company, for example, while she gets the name of a great contact for raising money for a community association she belongs to.

Indeed, a general goal you should set for yourself in every networking contact is to find something out about the other person. You should leave networking conversations knowing something new about them, either about their additional business lines, trends affecting their business, or some of the challenges they are facing. The exchange of information may or may not lead to an immediate payoff. Relationships take time to nurture, and one doesn't enter every relationship looking for something of immediate economic value. *Don't measure your networking by its economic utility or the immediacy of the payback.*

How Not to Measure Networking

Networking should not be based on pure exchange. I routinely receive phone calls from people who want to meet to discuss a potentially "mutually rewarding relationship." This often leaves me feeling queasy. Perhaps I would have been quite happy to meet with this person – not to satisfy some need of my own, but simply to help him. The promise of a mutually rewarding relationship completely undermines this desire to be helpful and removes any motivation to make further contact. I also find it extremely presumptuous for someone I don't know to "know" what would be good for me.

If you are looking for help, don't sugarcoat it by implying you are doing the other person as much of a favor as they are doing for you.

Types of Networkers

The robotic networker: Erica C. was invited to a get-together with a group of talented and accomplished women from a broad range of professional fields. While the other women were having animated discussions, punctuated by gales of laughter, about everything under the sun, from work and careers to relationships and children to pure gossip, Erica was going around collecting business cards. "That was great," she told her hostess at the end of the evening. "I've got 15 business cards!" Erica was concerned only to identify potential resources to assist her with work-related problems. If she had allowed herself to participate in the spirit of the evening, she could have learned much that could enrich her *life* as well as her career.

The information interviewer: "I'm currently exploring my career options. I'd like to meet with you and learn about what you do." Everyone gets these calls. We've been getting them ever since the job-search gurus began to advocate "information interviewing" as a strategy for making contacts and positioning oneself for opportunities ("I'd really appreciate if you could critique my résumé . . ."). This was once an ingenious notion: most people like to be helpful, after all, and are usually flattered to be asked for advice. But it's a strategy that's getting tired. People have heard it too often.

Most people today don't have the luxury of time to meet face to face with each caller. At best, they may be able to spend some time on the phone. Information-seekers who insist on a face-to-face meeting will usually be disappointed. And trust me, the promise of a free lunch is not going to make a meeting more likely.

If you are seeking information, be mindful of the other person's time. One strategy is to make contact by e-mail. This grants the recipient more control over when, if ever, to deal with your request. But don't let the ease of transmitting e-mail lead you into besieging your contacts with a lot of information, or requiring them to take an inordinate amount of time responding. If you hope to get a useful response, be targeted. (And if you get a response, make sure you thank the person afterward!)

The incessant networker: Recently I was telling a client how I avoid talking to fellow passengers on airplanes. He was horrified, asking, "But what if the person sitting next to you was a potential client?" I admire entrepreneurial zeal as much as the next person. But you don't have to approach every interaction as a potential business lead.

The out-of-left-field networker: The caller says, "Hello, this is Jill. I'm in the process of changing my career direction, and I'd like your opinion. You were so helpful before . . ." And you wonder: "Who the hell is Jill?"

When you're calling someone you haven't seen or spoken to in years, don't assume the person will instantly remember you — particularly if the previous encounter was fleeting. If in doubt, provide some clues as you initiate the conversation so the other person can recall you ("Hello, this is Jill Smith. You may not remember me, but I'm a friend of Fred Jones and we met . . ."). Don't overestimate your own importance in your contacts' lives.

The narrow networker: It's amazing how parochial some people are in their networking. Bankers hang out with bankers, accountants with accountants, programmers with programmers. As a result, they develop a very narrow view of the world. In today's work world, where *breadth* is an increasingly key requirement for career success, expanding your network horizons will increase your understanding of critical business and social trends. Developing a broad network of contacts both inside your workplace and outside it – for example by participating in professional associations, social-interest groups, and community organizations – gives you a broader perspective on your work, as well as enriching your life.

Moreover, even from a purely practical point of view, it makes little sense to network only with people in your profession or industry. If there is a downturn in your area, you could find yourself in a network of people all looking for the same kind of work. Getting involved in multiple networks will increase your exposure to potential opportunities if you need to make a career transition.

Networking as Good Social Relations

The best networkers I know are conscious of the other person in the equation. They know what that person needs or values. They take genuine pleasure in doing something that makes a small difference in the other person's life. They are willing to spend a little extra effort helping out, and they don't begrudge the time they spend helping. Neither do they view it as a *quid pro quo.*

Communicating
on Fast Forward

A group of senior managers met for hours, developing a series of recommendations. The next day, when a copy of the recommendations was circulated among the members of the group, there was widespread consternation. "I don't remember agreeing to *that*," said one manager. Another asked, "Are you sure we were at the same meeting?"

Communication breakdown. It's become something of an epidemic these days. Lately it seems that we're all too busy and preoccupied to communicate clearly, or to listen to what other people are trying to tell us.

How often these days do you make a phone call, only to hear the other person tapping away on a keyboard or clicking a mouse – or even *eating* – as they talk? When attention is diluted like this, both the task at hand *and* the quality of the communication suffer.

Even when people appear to be taking part in a dialogue, their minds are often elsewhere. You are just one of five thousand things competing for their attention. They're thinking, "I'm exhausted, my boss is breathing down my neck, my partner is pissed off because she hasn't seen me in two weeks, my kid has three studs in his nose. I really don't have time to pay attention to you."

When I'm talking to people I often have the feeling that they really don't want to listen because in their minds the inevitable result will simply be more things to do — more to e-mail, fax, delegate, or report on — as if they don't have enough to do already.

An Escalation in Hyperbole

Given how difficult it has become to capture anyone's attention for more than a nanosecond, it's not surprising that there has been a steady escalation in hyperbole. It's no longer enough to say that something is "interesting" or "quite good" or "notable." Instead we have to throw around adjectives like the titles of old science-fiction magazines. Either something is the most extraordinary, amazing, astounding, and fantastic idea, book, theory, or event since the dawn of civilization, or it's hardly worth considering.

And then there are the miscommunications that occur when people working in overdrive leap to conclusions. Too impatient to process an entire communication, they fixate on key words or phrases, trying to speed-read the meaning. Metaphorically, they become like teenagers rolling their eyes at nagging parents, insisting that they *get the point* when they don't really get it at all.

This rush to get to the point — even the *wrong* point — is certainly understandable. But you wouldn't want your surgeon to skim over the results of your x-rays, or your lawyer to surf through the fine print. The consequences of not listening carefully — whether to a friend, a colleague, a boss, or a family member — can be equally disastrous.

Then again, even when you listen carefully, the other person may not really be saying anything. How often these days do you hear someone lapsing into "yadda, yadda, yadda"? It's as if we can't be bothered, or are too tired, to take the time to actually *think* about the content of the information — or else afraid that our listeners are too restless and bored and impatient to listen to any details. Instead we go through the *motions* of having communi-cated, skimming the surface rather than immersing ourselves in the content of the information.

And even when we *do* appear to be providing information, we are often only exchanging what are really meaningless abstractions: "globalization," "impact of technology," "profound cultural change," and so on. These are merely headings for whole pages of hypertext yet to be properly discussed, or even thought about. For all the meaning this impatient short-hand conveys, we might just as well be saying, "yadda, yadda, yadda."

The irony, of course, is that communication skills have never been at a greater premium. Given the pace of work and the tremendous amount of information to be exchanged and processed, it's crucial to be able to communicate effectively. Moreover, the new configuration of the workplace, and in particular the growing emphasis on project work, compels us to communicate in new ways. Members of a project team, for example, must be able to establish rapport quickly and build relationships with people they may never have met before – and in some cases may never meet face to face. And they must communicate clearly with people from different disciplines across borders and time zones.

Improving Communication

Traditional management-development courses in communication, with their focus on skills such as good listening, clarification, feedback, and being nonjudgmental, remain valuable and worthwhile. But at the same time they largely miss the most fundamental point: How do you connect with someone when you are just one of a multitude of things competing for their attention?

There are no easy answers to this question. But there are, at least, some strategies that improve your chances of being not only heard but understood. You need to be able to communicate in a way that is both *graphic* and *to the point*. Ask yourself:

- Can I quickly capture my listener's attention and get my message across?
- Can I use words to paint a picture, tell a story, make information vivid? Can I talk in headlines?
- Can I write clearly, persuasively, and with impact?
- Can I zero in on key concepts and translate them appropriately for my listener's requirements? Or do I embellish needlessly and bury vital points in useless information?
- Am I aware of what my listener is interested in – as opposed to what I feel a need to say?
- Can I quickly establish relationships and credibility with people I've never met?

At the same time, think about the kind of behaviors you are demonstrating both as a communicator and as a listener. Are you contributing to the hysterical din of miscommunication, or are you taking the time both to understand and to make yourself understood?

It's very easy to fall into the trap of thinking you have heard something before, when this time it has a different twist. Pay attention carefully to what you are hearing and make sure you can summarize the essence of what you have just heard.

If you're not really hearing something that somebody else is saying, be honest. Tell the person that you're overloaded and you'd prefer to deal with it at some other point. It's better to admit you haven't fully processed something than to do the other person the disservice of pretending to listen. You may have missed something important that they really needed you to hear.

In a faster-paced world, we will increasingly be working with people we've never met, or who come from different disciplines. Given the shape of work to come, and the growing complexity of communications, the ability to communicate powerfully and persuasively, and to decode what others are trying to tell you, will be critical to career success.

"Don't Take
This Personally, But . . ."

"*D*o you mind if I give you some feedback?" How often, when asked this question, do you really want to say, "Well actually, I do." But in an era when we are all supposed to be continuously learning, we worry that this would reflect an underlying defensiveness.

Well, the reasons one might be less than enamored of receiving such *unsolicited* feedback are simple enough. (Note that we are not talking about a formal coaching situation where there is a meaningful expectation that your behavior will be helpfully assessed by someone else.)

Unsolicited Feedback

To begin with, when people ask, "Do you want feedback?", almost invariably what they really mean is, "I'd like to criticize you." After all, if they were going to praise you, would they ask for permission? And in that statement, "I'd like to criticize you," they are making two major assumptions.

First, they are assuming that they know something that you don't already know — that they can tell you something significant about your behavior that you were not aware of, and that their opinion counts for something. In fact, by the time most people are in their 30s, they have fairly accurate insight into their own behavior. It is unusual that someone can make an off-the-cuff observation about a problem behavior that you are completely unaware of. So if you have just made a complete idiot of yourself, you probably already know that, and don't necessarily need the point to be driven home any further. As one person commented, "I'm 40 years old and I've been doing presentations for 15 years now. When I've completely missed it, I usually already know."

Another assumption is that you will benefit from the feedback – that the behavior being commented on is *something you can change*. Some behaviors are changeable. But given the relative consistency of personality characteristics, the chances are that if you continue to exhibit this area of so-called weakness for a long time, you are probably aware of the difficulty. You have either tried to change it without success, or else focused on improving in other areas.

Unsolicited feedback is also often essentially trivial in nature. It's as if people feel an expectation they *should* give you feedback, so they make a comment on the smallest detail in order to say anything at all.

One woman, for example, had just delivered a successful sales presentation on which she had worked long and hard. Her efforts paid off and her company stole the account from a competitor. Her boss's comment was, "On the fifth slide, you misspelled the word 'people.'" True enough, she thought, but in the bigger scheme of things, would it not have made more sense to have said, "Congratulations, great presentation, and by the way, on a very minor note for your future reference, you had a typo . . ."?

Often this focus on tiny details says more about their own need to puff up their self-importance than it does about you. What is particularly galling is that such comments are typically purely *descriptive* ("You look really tired") rather than *prescriptive*, making suggestions as to what you could do differently.

"Don't Take It Personally"

And then there's that old chestnut, "Don't take it personally." Janice, for example, as part of what she described as a "group dump masquerading as team-building," was told that she was "rude, arrogant, and condescending." She asked the group, in a somewhat sarcastic manner, "Is there anything else you would like to share with me?", only to be told, "Don't be defensive, you're not supposed to take it personally . . ."

You have to wonder, if someone is being criticized, who owns that behavior, the world or that person? Experts on communication will insist that it is your behavior that is being criticized, not you as a person. Indeed, this is one of the fundamental precepts of performance appraisals. But the behavior is grounded in the individual. How else should Janice take it if not personally?

One especially nasty variation of feedback is what an organizational consultant colleague of mine calls "the s___-filled Twinkie . . . ," in which criticism comes with a perfunctory sugarcoating. For example, "I really liked the way you answered questions in that presentation. Unfortunately, I don't think your content showed the level of preparation I expect of you. But good job on the Q&A."

All this said, it's true that people will often *say* they want feedback, when in fact they don't like it at all. As part of my Ph.D. thesis I did research on how people respond to praise and criticism from their bosses. The situations described real-life events such as writing a report or giving a presentation with the boss providing behavioral feedback. For example, "You captured the key concepts in a vivid and compelling manner," versus "I think you could have got to the key points faster."

My research showed when people were praised, their moods or emotions were significantly altered in a positive manner. When given negative feedback, even so-called helpful and constructive feedback, they reacted with anger, disappointment, and confusion.

So when people say they want feedback, what they often really want is unqualified admiration and affirmation.

Individual Differences

There are significant differences in how people respond to feedback. Some people are more sensitive to criticism, while others are more dispassionate and capable of shrugging it off. For example, some people, when told that their report is "quite good," hear "your report was a disaster." Or, after having given a presentation that 90% of participants described as "excellent" and 10% said "needs improvement," some will focus obsessively on the minority opinion. On the other hand, there are those who fail to recognize even the most damning criticism.

Some people are simply more sensitive to, and more strongly affected by, the way others see them. They feel better about themselves to the extent that they've been praised. They are quicker to pick up subtle interpersonal cues related to others' reactions to them — for example, that their listeners look bored, or that their joke died.

Other people are less sensitive, even impervious, to how the world sees them. They are less likely to pick up cues and are also less affected by negative feedback.

Some think that people whose feelings about themselves are more easily affected by how others see them must have low self-esteem. But in my experience, people who are more sensitive are just as likely as their less-sensitive counterparts to see themselves as being capable and effective, and are not particularly more prone to depression — in fact, they are equally optimistic in their expectations of the world.

Giving Feedback

What is true of unsolicited feedback is just as true of the feedback you may get through such official mechanisms as performance appraisal or coaching and counseling situations. Most people resent getting negative feedback from their boss or team leader — all the more so if their compensation or prospects for advancement are at stake.

Organizations continue to spend millions of dollars constantly revising their performance appraisal systems. But the sad fact remains that, no matter how couched the comments may be, most people don't like negative feedback. Although in the long term people may actually benefit from it, don't be surprised that they are less than enthusiastic to hear it right now.

The following principles will increase the probability that the person getting the feedback will actually benefit from it:

- Remember to describe the positive. People are usually more aware of their faults than strengths, so don't emphasize the negative at the expense of the positive.
- Show how something could have been done differently. Focus on behaviors that can be changed.
- Consider extenuating circumstances. For example, "I know you've been under a lot of pressure lately, so your recent performance may reflect the fact that you are really tired. However, in the future . . ."
- Don't insist that the other person share your views of their relative inadequacies. You are entitled to an opinion on their behavior, but you don't have the right to demand that they agree with your assessment.
- People are often aware of faults. Articulating them can motivate them to change, as long as it isn't soul destroying.
- Tailor your feedback in relation to the person's personality, remembering that some people are more sensitive to criticism than others.
- Check out whether your feedback is truly wanted.

The Politics
of Bad Fit

Rebecca, a three-year employee of an advertising agency, had been put on probation as a result of a number of performance problems: she did not follow through on commitments, failed to deliver projects on time, and was ill-prepared for important meetings. Weekly conscientious coaching sessions with her manager improved her performance significantly.

Still, her boss, Eric, remained unhappy. He acknowledged that the performance issues had been addressed, and that Rebecca was now following through on her assignments and performing well.

"The real problem is I just don't like her," he said. "I find her silly, I can't stand her fake laugh, she's always dropping by my office, and it's driving me crazy. And yet I realize that many people find her very charming, so this may be as much of a statement about myself and what I like in people as it is about her. So I don't know where to go from here. Where do you draw the line between where it is acceptable for management to intervene and asking someone to change their basic personality?"

Authentically Obnoxious

This is indeed a thorny problem. Organizations like to flatter themselves in believing that almost everything an individual does in the workplace can be described and commented on in behavioral terms – and that individuals with problems can be coached for performance improvement. But the reality is that when people come to work, they bring their whole personalities with them. And that whole personality, in some cases, will cause some people to cringe. They are too loud, pushy, manipulative, political, dense, and so on.

We like to believe that today's organizations celebrate diversity and individual differences. People are supposed to be freer to bring their authentic selves to work. But what if that authentic self is objectionable?

Of course, annoying habits or distasteful characteristics are essentially a *subjective* question rather than something that can be *objectively* described and corrected. What one person finds unattractive, another might actually like. Organizational culture also plays a part in determining what is acceptable. A brash, aggressive person might flourish in sales but get on people's nerves in a research department.

Organizations cannot legislate desirable personality characteristics, nor do they have the right to change them. And yet problems of clashing personalities are ubiquitous and can often lead to dysfunctional or toxic work environments.

Managers like Eric wonder: How do you comment on such behaviors? Do you even have the right to comment on them? They often feel embarrassed having to "muck about" in such potentially emotive areas. Traditionally, these matters are seen as lying outside the realms of acceptable feedback. On the other hand, these behaviors not only may be irritating to co-workers, they may also significantly interfere with the person's effectiveness and advancement.

Michael, for example, had to deal with a subordinate who wanted to move into management, but whose abrasive manner made the move impossible. Without a change of style, the individual was told, he would not achieve his goals. No one likes to hear this kind of information, but it was useful feedback all the same.

Saving Face

One way that organizations can manage these situations is by referring people to coaches. Coaches have the interpersonal sensitivity and the psychological skills to describe the questionable behavior and its impact on others in a way that allows the individual to save face. And the coach can provide clear descriptions of alternative behaviors.

Coaching can be particularly helpful when the behavior is experienced by others in a way that is not intended by the individual. Very shy people, for example, may come across as arrogant and contemptuous of their team members when in fact they are simply socially uncomfortable.

It should be recognized, though, that coaching is far from a panacea. Some people simply lack any insight into their behavior, or its impact on others, and not even the most skillful coach can bring them to recognize the source of their problems. Other people don't *want* to change: they like themselves just the way they are and think it's the people around them who have the problem, not they. And in at least some cases, they are right.

Where an individual is unwilling or unable to change, there are really only a few options. You can learn to live with what you experience as obnoxious behavior. You can move away from the problem person — requesting a transfer, or finding another job. Or, if you are in a position to do so, you can fire the person.

However, one would be hard-pressed to make a legal case for firing someone for talking too loudly, having an irritating laugh, or being too political. That's why irreconcilable personality conflicts are usually dealt with quietly:

the individual is shown the door as part of a "restructuring" or because — using that favorite managerial chestnut — they are a "bad fit."

Indeed, we often use such euphemisms as "style," "culture," "chemistry," or "fit" to describe these situations. But the reality is that when we say someone had a problem fitting into the culture, it's usually just a polite way of saying that we don't like them.

A Matter of Style?

A whole other category of conflicts surrounds the question of personal taste and style. Is it all right to come to work wearing nose rings? Eyebrow rings? Visible tattoos? This is becoming a major source of intergenerational conflict in the workplace.

Styles and tastes change over time: just a decade ago, the idea that men in business suits would wear earrings would have seemed utterly fantastic to most people. But there are still boundaries set by prevailing cultural norms. You can push the edges of the envelope, but you still have to be able to get *into* the envelope.

How free we really are to be ourselves is a complex issue today, when many think of their life as a work of art that they are creating. Looking down the road, the impact of personal style issues on the workplace is likely to be magnified.

Teenagers have always celebrated personal style in their identification with a particular subculture, be it hippie, street, or preppie. But today we are witnessing an unprecedented number of subcultures or "tribes" among teenagers, who are adopting the dress, mannerisms, music, and style of their preferred subculture at an increasingly early age — and defending their memberships aggressively as anti-corporate punk-rockers, party-loving ravers, materialistic preppies, or whatever else.

These kids are growing up with a belief that expressing their personal style is their right, their entitlement. When they enter the workplace, will they make the kind of transitions that their boomer parents did and be prepared to grow up, build a career, and conform?

Or will they simply become the obnoxious person in the next cubicle?

Recession-Proofing
Your Career

*T*here's a recession coming. There's *always* a recession coming, sooner or later. Is your career recession-proof?

Let's be clear. We are *not* talking here about the security of your current job, because these days no job is secure. Even through the boom years, organizations continued to restructure and downsize to become ever-more effective and competitive. Another downturn in the business cycle will only accelerate the pace of change — and make careful career management even more crucial.

These days, as discussed throughout this book, no matter what our official employment status, we are all temporary workers. Whether we have a conventional full-time job, or are contingent, contract, or freelance workers, we are all living and working in TempWorld. In TempWorld everything shifts rapidly. Nothing is forever, everything is temporary: where you work, what you do there, the skills you use, the people you work with.

In this fast-shifting world, there can be no guarantees attached to any particular job. But there is much that you can do to insulate yourself from change and economic upheaval, by equipping yourself with the skills to manage your career more effectively. And what that involves is becoming a *career activist*.

Hillary, a 27-year-old systems analyst, quit her job to study French for six months. Longer term, she wants to be able to parlay her information technology skills into work with an international organization.

Zack, 30, a conference producer, is devoting all of his free time away from work to networking with consultants as well as furiously saving his money. Next year, he hopes to become a ghost writer for management consultants.

Forty-year-old Jane has just sold her home in downtown Toronto and moved to a small town. She is using the proceeds from her house to subsidize her pursuit of a law degree.

Twenty-five-year-old Peter does not have a business card. He chose to work for an international petrochemical company as a contractor because of its reputation for attracting top talent and doing leading-edge work. He's managed to stretch out a six-month contract into two years, acquiring important business skills, by understudying pregnant women and then taking over from them when they go on maternity leave.

Taking Charge of Careers

Each of these people, in their different ways, has become a career activist. Instead of taking a passive approach to their work they have *taken charge* of their careers, organizing their lives to ensure their long-term career and personal interests are met.

Being a career activist means stepping back from the frenzy of daily business to reflect on what you are doing, why you are doing it, and whether it meets your short- and long-term needs. It means taking the long view of your career, rather than only taking your "career temperature" when you feel a chill.

Let's look at some of the rules for this new world of work:

Ensure your employability: If you lost your main source of income tomorrow, could you find an alternate source to replace it? How do you evaluate the currency of your skills? By the standards set by your current employer? Or by wider industry and professional standards?

Do you actively pursue learning and development opportunities, including ones that will stretch you? Can you describe one important thing you have learned over the past six months and one that you will be acquiring in the next? The more you learn, the more options you have.

The most important imperative in protecting yourself now and in the future is ensuring that you have *choices*. Don't let yourself be held back by a lack of skill portability ("I've been working for this company so long, I'll never be able to get another job"), or fear of change.

All too often I meet people who have been good performers in their own organization who have discovered that they are in effect stuck. Because they have become so closely identified with a particular company or industry, their skills are not perceived as being readily transferable to other settings. Measure yourself against community as well as internal standards. Your professional association and network can assist you.

Have a fallback position — develop a new mind-set: Human resource manager Carol K. works for a large public utility. Anticipating the impact of regulatory changes in her industry, she is pursing a diploma in alternative dispute resolution. "I know my job may be vulnerable," she said. "This way, if the worst happens, I can always hang out a shingle as a conflict mediator."

Don't put all your eggs in one basket. If you limit yourself to one particular area or sector, you limit your opportunities, too. Today it is critical to have multiple options, multiple avenues, and multiple roles. If you only see yourself, for example, in the role of an employee, your work options are significantly more limited than if you understand how your skills can be applied in different types of employment relationships in different sectors and industries. Having a fallback position means that you can equally see yourself selling your skills as a contract worker, as a freelance consultant, or as a small-business owner, even if these other roles are less desirable to you than that of full-time employee. In other words, redefine the way in which you work, and your relationship to potential purchasers of your skills and knowledge, to ensure your future employability. This means developing a new mind-set.

Know your key skills — think Lego: We've all heard the statement that in the future we will hold five to seven careers. When I discuss this in workshops, many people find it alarming. They think it means they are without substance, with no enduring value, programmed to self-destruct every few years. They fear they will be required to constantly reinvent themselves.

Actually, most people will not be embarking on entirely new careers (architect becomes farmer) so much as *reconfiguring* existing skills and experience in new ways (architect hobby farmer starts business designing and building greenhouses).

The first step in career management is to know your underlying or core skills. Like a child's Lego pieces, these are the building blocks that you can continually reassemble, though in slightly new configurations, as you move through your career. Identifying your key strengths and skills requires going through a rigorous self-assessment. Ask yourself, what are your unique talents, what are the special skills you bring to the table?

Develop a work identity independent of your job, defining yourself by what you do rather than simply by your job title. Look at yourself as the owner of a self-managed group of skills and abilities that you can apply in a wide range of jobs and projects. For example, 29-year-old chartered accountant John D. put it this way, "If I see myself as a financial professional with strong technical experience in telecommunications and effective team-building and leadership skills, currently leasing my knowledge to ABC Company, I have significantly more mobility than if my whole work identity is tied to my professional designation."

Prepare for areas of competence, not jobs: A global marketplace means jobs come and go as quickly as changes in the stock market. Today's hottest jobs may not exist tomorrow. Some people, worried about their employability, are responding to current, much-trumpeted predictions of a severe shortage of information technology workers by enrolling in Information Technology courses. If you love computers, then this work represents a great choice. But don't enter a field just because you think that's where the hot jobs are. To begin with that work may not exist. But even if it does, it may not represent a good match with your own skills and abilities. Start with an assessment of your own strengths and interests, then look to see where you may match up best in the job market.

Instead of preparing yourself for specific jobs, think in terms of the areas in which you want to contribute, whether it be technical areas such as software design or market analysis, or non-technical areas such as team-building, leadership of knowledge workers, or relationship-building.

Market! Market! Market! In the new workplace, people must perform at an exceedingly high level *now*, while at the same time always marketing for the *future* – keeping one eye on the next work assignment and positioning themselves for it.

This leads some people to wonder, "If I'm spending all my time marketing, how can I be producing at the same time?" But marketing yourself doesn't mean endlessly parading your list of credentials and accomplishments to the world at large. It does mean letting other key people know about your skills and how they can add value. Do you keep potential clients informed of significant accomplishments and how they can be applied to meeting their needs? Do you cultivate and maintain an active network both inside your profession and outside it?

You need to be continuously networking, but in a *thoughtful* way. That means building *knowledge networks*, not simply handing out business cards or e-mail addresses at business or association meetings. Good networkers are "wired." Their networks are broad, ranging well beyond their own professional boundaries. They cultivate relationships with people who know how to get things done. They know who to go to for information or referrals or plum work assignments.

Good networkers above all leave an impression on you because they have engaged your attention and listened to you as if what you had to say was interesting and important.

If you are uncomfortable in face-to-face networking, develop alternative strategies. For example, if you have something to say, you can become known as an expert in a particular field by writing articles for trade magazines, speaking at professional events, setting up your own web page, or chairing a professional conference.

It can be argued, in fact, that in today's hyperkinetic business environment, in which potential clients are too busy just to be schmoozed, being able to give people hard information that they can use will be much more desirable.

Develop *long-term relationships* with people. In the future, increasingly, we will be moving back and forth between different employers, and you may well find yourself five years down the road working for a previous employer. Treat everyone with whom you work – whether a boss, co-worker, customer, or client – as a potential client.

Learn to walk a delicate line between bugging people and being responsive to their information-overloaded minds.

Act Type A, but Be Type B: The Type A, hard-driving, achievement-oriented, coronary-prone behavior style used to be *the* model for success in our society. And in the current economic environment, the Type-A individual's focus, commitment, stamina, and excessive achievement-orientation may continue to be highly desired assets.

As executive recruiter Susannah Kelly of Herman Smith International observes, "Today, you must perform in a way that exceeds expectations, not just meets them. In these volatile times, to just meet expectations means you are in maintenance mode, not in change or leadership mode."

Work-intoxicated Type A's may well be better able to sustain these intense productivity pressures than their more relaxed Type B counterparts. So we need to *Act Type A.*

But at the same time, the work world we are living is far more thankless than it used to be. We don't get the kind of rewards, compliments, and positive feedback we used to because everyone's too busy. Moreover, there will typically be periods where employment is interrupted, and we have no work in which to play out our achievement-strivings. This is bad news for Type A's, whose whole sense of self is tied to doing, performing, achieving, and acting. So we also have to *Think Type B* – able to feel good about ourselves both when we are producing and when we are not, both when it is recognized and when it is not. That means cultivating a sense of self that is not completely tied to our achievements and accomplishments.

Cultivate emotional resilience: Can you withstand disappointment, juggle stressful situations, and handle pressure with aplomb? In today's workplace, do you have the resilience to deal with failures as well as successes? Can you learn from those failures so that you are not immobilized by them but can use them to your advantage in the future? Successful people reflect on things that didn't go well in an honest way, but they don't beat themselves up for it, endlessly revisiting the event.

Stay culturally current: I'm frequently amazed at how culturally parochial so many senior business and professional people are. Given the complex economic, cultural, and demographic global environment in which we operate, it is critical to stay tuned to larger cultural trends that affect the landscape and context of work.

Do you read outside your professional milieu? This means reading broadly, whether it be book reviews, international business magazines, non-fiction in areas related to general social trends, magazines such as *Fast Company* and *Rolling Stone*, alternative press digests such as *Utne Reader*, or going on-line to participate in discussion groups. Stay in tune with pop culture and be engaged by viewpoints from different sectors of the economy and demographic groups. World and cultural events have a direct impact on your work.

Try to glean from these sources important trends that will affect how your work is carried out, new potential applications, sources of competition, and customs. Never before has public opinion played such an important role in day-to-day political and business decision-making.

Sometimes, older people tell me they feel discriminated against because of their age. While that certainly happens, I find that often these individuals are somewhat disconnected from the world around them. Being in the know – in tune with the *Zeitgeist* – is important for being able to establish personal relationships with others, as well as for managing your career effectively.

Be a compelling communicator: Every time you talk to someone today you are competing with five thousand other priorities against a background of almost chronic sleep deprivation.

Our hit-the-ground-running culture means that today we must immediately establish credibility with co-workers, clients, and project members without benefit of what was once the "getting to know someone and exchanging pleasantries" stage. The person you are communicating or working with today may also be halfway around the world and/or from a different discipline. Can you translate what you do in a way that someone who doesn't share your professional expertise will readily understand?

Manage your finances: The most important source of protection we can have is knowing that we are not "owned" by debt. Given the temporary nature of the future of work, we cannot make any assumptions about employment continuity, nor can we make any assumptions about income continuity. Ensure that your finances are in order so that you're not gripped by fear of a downturn in the economy.

If you lost your job or a major client tomorrow, do you have enough money in the bank to tide you over until you replace them? Are you doing the work you choose to do, or is your work governed by fear of economic instability? Are you making significant personal sacrifices to maintain a standard of living?

Perhaps we can take a lesson here from many of the post-boomers. Having grown up in a period of economic instability, and with no illusions of any corporate or government pension plan being available to provide for them adequately in their senior years, many of them are already aggressive savers.

We can take a lesson, too, from the generations of immigrants who came to North America with little more than the clothes on their back. *Thinking like an immigrant* means understanding the importance of having *multiple income streams* whether from a business, renting out a basement apartment, owning vending machines, or giving violin lessons. We can no longer afford to rely on all of our income coming from one source. Whether you are a full-time employee or an independent contractor, cultivate other sources of income as an invaluable fallback in difficult times.

Act like an insider, think like an outsider: There is a paradox in contemporary business. Management gurus wax lyrical about thinking independently, being inventive, "thinking out of the box." But most large organizations place a heavy and in many cases contradictory emphasis on teamwork and group solidarity.

I have met people who have spent so much time in an organization that they have lost the "I." Ask them a question about how they think or feel about something and they immediately respond, "Well, at the ACME Company, *we* do *x* . . . ," as if the way their company does it is justification of the value of that activity and behavior.

Managing your career effectively requires balancing these apparently mutually competitive imperatives. In a teamwork environment, you need to be able to work effectively in groups. But at the same time you need to be able to work independently and to evaluate the team's work from an external perspective, rising above the "group think" in which it is so easy to become mired.

Some organizations mouth the rhetoric of "thinking independently" but actually want to customize everything to reflect their own internal corporate values and culture. If you find yourself routinely using jargon that only someone who works in your company or work team understands, you may be losing your capacity to think independently.

As a general rule, successful people get involved in teamwork very judiciously. They recognize that teamwork can be extremely valuable where the combined talents of a group can deliver a better product than an individual working alone. But they don't regard this way of working as good for its own sake, nor do they value consensus achieved at any cost.

Being able to think independently will become even more important as people are increasingly forced to make quick decisions without benefit of group input. People often become successful, in fact, because they didn't know how things "should" be done. Without the benefit of building on accumulated wisdom, they have invented their own solutions.

Be capable of rewarding yourself: You need to be able to give yourself the pat on the back for a job well done – the chances are good that no one else will take the time to notice. Be realistic in your expectations, celebrate your successes, and learn how to nourish yourself. Don't define your worth only in terms of your measurable accomplishments. Do you punish yourself for things that don't work out? Can you live with less than perfect? Do you celebrate your own success?

The ability to celebrate your successes, and *know* you *deserve* to celebrate them, may well be the most important skill of all.

Conclusion:
The Good News About Careers

Doug has just taken a job with a company he describes as having a reputation for being a career killer, "chewing people up and spitting them out." When asked why he would possibly commit career hara-kiri by joining such an organization, he says, "I'll be getting much more out of this than they will – moving to another city, being exposed to a new industry, and learning a very hot new technology. And if it doesn't work out, we'll just rent a U-Haul, load it up, and try something else."

Sheila and Joe are a husband-and-wife team who started a very successful advertising agency. They have just entered into a strategic partnership with another agency, which gives that agency the option to buy them out. When asked what they would do if presented with an offer, Sheila says, "We'd travel in Asia for a year, and while we are traveling decide on a new business. I have no idea what that business might be, but I know we'll be successful at whatever we do."

Louise, a marketing manager, has just been downsized out of a job for the third time. "The first time it happened, I was shocked and scared," she says. "I thought I had done something wrong. I thought I would never find work again. Now I know the drill. In fact, this time I saw it coming and I welcomed it, because the settlement will buy me time to finish my MBA and move on to a new chapter in my life."

We have seen some sweeping changes in the world of work over the past decade. In my previous book, *Career Intelligence*, I looked at the impact of these changes on people's lives. Many people have suffered profoundly the end of job security; the loss of identification with a supposedly benevolent and all-protective organization; and the tremendous increase in both the pace and volume of work. Some people are still reeling from these changes. But for many others, time has been a healer. These people have come to recognize that many of the new work realities actually provide tremendous opportunities. There are in fact at least as many positives as negatives about the shape of the new career – *if* you are able to respond to the new work realities in a creative way, taking responsibility for managing your own career.

The Armies of the Day

When I started my career working at a large petrochemical company, I watched armies of brown- and black-suited women and men pouring in through the giant portals each morning. In my mind's eye, I always imagined row upon row of employee lockers lining the grand lobby, each identified by an employee number. The workers would go to their lockers to hang up their personality, sexuality, and anything else that made them real as human beings. They would emerge in full corporate mask, ready to meet the day head on.

We have lived through the breakdown of these old-style corporate monoliths with their rigid bureaucracy, ossified roles and policies, and clearly defined expectations of "how things are done around here." Marxists once insisted that the state would wither away after a communist revolution. That didn't happen. But there *has* been a revolution in the world of work.

Traditional organizations, if not quite withering away, have been profoundly transformed. At the same time, new organizations have emerged with very different corporate cultures. The result? The creation of a much more diverse world of work. This new world is potentially liberating for the individual, offering much greater opportunities for empowerment and self-expression. It is much more in tune with individual needs and personal characteristics.

So let's look at some of the *good* news about careers.

The End of Paternalism

In the old world of work, the relationship between the individual and the organization was characterized by fear and insecurity. The company was all-knowing and all-powerful. If you did what was required of you, the organization would reward you with advancement and salary increases, guiding you along a clearly marked career path towards your ultimate destiny.

Old-style organizations were benevolent in their own way, providing job security, benefits, and developmental experiences. But the relationship was one-sided. The price of corporate success was conformity and a permanent state of dependence.

Today there is a new relationship between the individual and his or her employer – a "new employment contract." Under this new deal, neither side is beholden to the other, and both sides understand that the relationship is based on *mutual exchange*. As a result, individuals are on a more equal footing with the organization. People no longer feel "owned" or enchained. They work because they *want* to contribute to the achievement of mutual goals.

This sort of relationship, of course, has to be earned and cultivated on both sides. As we have seen, for their part, organizations need to provide individuals with the tools to manage their own careers in the light of the new work realities. Only when people are empowered by a belief in their own employability can they develop a more equal, rather than fear-driven, relationship to their organization.

Individuals, meanwhile, increasingly recognize their responsibility in managing their own careers. They understand that they no longer can rely on a benevolent organization to do it for them. And we see this happening. People are taking a stand on what they want from their work. At the extremes, the formerly beholden individual may even be seen as cocky. When they are not saying, "Show me the money," they are saying, "Show me the learning, show me the opportunity."

In the new world of work, you have the freedom to choose your work, your colleagues, your clients, your workspace. Employers used to be the buyers. Now they have to do a selling job. Individuals ask, "Why should I work here, what will I learn, what will I walk out with at the end of the day that I didn't have before?" If the organization tries to sell them a bill of goods, they are quite willing to walk away.

Forty-one-year-old Glenna, an accomplished independent consultant, was hired to facilitate a company's two-day off-site team-building event. After the fifth meeting with her clients reviewing her design for the event line by line, she said, "You hired me because I am a professional, and presumably you thought I could do the work. But I'm too old for this. If you can't trust me to work at the level I've been contracted to, then find yourself another consultant."

If one word can be used to characterize the new career, it is *self-reliance*. That means you believe in your own competence and can deal with all the uncertainties associated with the new work world, because you know you have the skills to sell and you know your own value. And you are ready and able to move on when necessary.

A recently survey by Royal Bank shows that about half of Canadians have an up-to-date résumé. Perhaps more than anything else, this shows that people truly understand the importance of being ready to move on, that they no longer hold a simple belief in secure employment.

When my son was born, I said to a friend, half jokingly, "I guess the choice is independence, or dependence. If I promote his independence, I have to fully expect him to be calling me from a different time zone when he is an adult." In the future, we will all be free agents, moving from work assignment to work assignment, city to city, country to country in pursuit of challenging and lucrative work. Greater mobility means greater opportunity. At the same time, we will need creativity to ensure that friendship, family, and a sense of community survive, and that our relationships are not virtual and digitally expressed, but are living, dynamic, and rooted.

The New Security

In the new workplace, contract workers and independent consultants work alongside people who still have traditional full-time jobs. But no matter what your official work status, there is no security other than that you create for yourself: the security of knowing you are employable in other work settings.

Indeed, many people who have made the transition from traditional employment to contract work or consulting report that they feel *more* security now than when they worked for an organization. Rather than waiting around passively for the axe to fall – to be fired, downsized, or restructured – they have become active players in managing their own lives.

As a marketing consultant puts it, "My life used to depend on the whims of my boss or the attitudes of consultants hired to reinvent the corporation. I was in a permanent state of anxiety. Now that I work for myself, I'm much less anxious, even though I frequently face times when I have no work."

Security today comes in a completely different package: no one can find complete protection from the vagaries of the marketplace, or the whims of employers. But what you can do is develop a mind-set that security lies in your own personal competence and effectiveness, and keep your repertoire of skills in line with market needs. You will then have the ultimate security: knowing that you are the principal player in what happens in your career and your life.

Freedom to Design Your Own Work

As the old monolithic corporate culture has fragmented, a new diversity in ways of working has emerged. When I was starting out my career, organizations typically made great protestations about their unique corporate culture, but there was in fact very little to distinguish between company A and company B. Today there is a much broader range of options in terms of work environments, and you can choose the one that best meets your needs.

If you want hip, find a small software developer where you can shoot pool on your break – and where *you* decide when you need or want a break. If you want collegiality, look for a team-focused environment. If you want freedom, work for yourself, telecommute, or find an employer who promotes individual autonomy. With a little research, you can *design your own work situation* to fit your own needs.

Before you can do this, though, you must first of all *know yourself*. Greater self-awareness means you can craft a work environment tailored to the "Five Ws," the critical determinants of what you are looking for in a work environment:

Who? What kinds of people do you want to work with and for? And what kinds of people interactions do you want to have? If, for example, you are more introverted, you may shy away from team-focused environments, preferring work that provides you with more time for one-on-one interactions and "back-room" work.

Why? Why do you work? What do you care about at this stage of your career? What are the core values you need to honor to feel good about yourself? If you have a young family, for example, you may decide to trade off a more challenging job that requires a lot of out-of-town travel for work that allows you to spend more time with your family. Of course, your values will change over time. In your 20s, for example, skill-building opportunities may be most important to you; in your 40s, you may be looking for work that enables you to give something back to the community.

What? What skills do you want to use and develop? That includes both *technical* skills — for example, software development, tax expertise, or designing training curriculum materials — and *general* skills, such as team-building, leading a group, and written communication. Some people who have very strong general skills may get more pleasure out of using these skills. For others, thinking about problems associated with their technical specialty is a key motivator in crafting a work environment.

Where? Increasingly, people are thinking about where they want to work, whether it be in a large metropolis or a small rural community, or even from home, via telecommuting. In some cases, in fact, people are telecommuting from a city across the country, with face-to-face contact kept to just two or three meetings a year.

As one human-resources professional recently e-mailed me, "For the first time in my professional life, I am telecommuting. I am thoroughly enjoying working from my ranch in Texas. Yesterday I was working at my dining-room table that sits in front of a huge picture window, when I discovered my two billy goats having quite an argument. I was just thinking how nice it is to be able to get my clothes out of the dryer while downloading my mail." This trend reaches right to the top. A recent newspaper article profiled a number of CEOs who were leading companies in countries other than where they lived.

When? We all vary in how many balls we want to juggle at any given time. If you get your energy from juggling several competing priorities, never quite having enough time to attend to everything, you will want to seek out a more fast-paced environment. If you are someone who prefers to work on a few things and put them to bed before going on to the next, you will want to look for a work environment and a way of working that will give you more control over your work.

Granted, it is nearly impossible today to find a *slow*-paced work environment, but with a little creativity you should be able to modify your work so that it better fits your needs. For example, you may choose telecommuting a couple of days a week to avoid the spontaneous distractions that occur as a result of ongoing office life. Or you might enjoy running a business where you're only working with a few clients at a time.

The good news is that the new business environment will increasingly be able to accommodate individual differences as people craft their work and work environment to play to their strengths and preferences. Instead of adapting yourself to fit an existing work environment, you can seek out a niche that fits you.

Competence Counts

As little as five years ago, one person in three would tell you a story about incompetent bosses with bloated egos enjoying long alcohol-fuelled lunches or networking on the golf course. You don't hear these stories nearly as often today. With the bar so high in business, and with organizations so flat, only the competent survive, and only the extremely competent thrive. The ability to *do* the work, add value, and be seen as adding value – not only by the people above you but also the people below you – is the most important determinant of success.

Competence counts, not titles: Merit, rather than who you know or how much experience you have, drives careers. Although some say that experience is the great teacher, it does not carry as much weight today. If someone says to you they have 20 years of experience, the question will be what *kind* of experience was it, good experience, bad experience, indifferent experience? What's important is what you have learned from that experience, and how you will express that learning in achieving results today.

Work is Fun: Business and Life Intermingle

Twenty-seven-year-old Tom K. borrowed $500 from his father and with two friends, a marketer and a recent design graduate from Ryerson Polytechnic University, developed a line of "streetwear" clothing, now being sold in the U.S. He did this without benefit of a marketing plan, an MBA, or a bank loan. "I'm part of this culture, I watch what my friends are wearing and listening to. I see what the Club Kids are doing. My inspiration comes from my life."

With the erosion of traditional boundaries that defined personal life and work life, people are enjoying their work more. They see work, like play, as an arena in which to express who they are. Indeed, as the boundaries between work and play break down, people increasingly describe their work as play. Work environments, too, have become more playful, especially in the newer high-tech startup organizations, where you can bring your dog to work, have a latte or a beer at 7 p.m., or go home and talk to a client while weeding your garden.

Life-Friendly Organizations

I talked on the telephone recently to four people in rapid succession. I was puzzled after I got off the phone with the fourth caller: there was something different about our conversation that I couldn't quite put my finger on. Then I realized what it was. In the background of the first three conversations was the sound of children. It was this "white noise" that I had missed when talking to the fourth caller. Increasingly, the sounds of life, whether it be dishes clinking or children playing, will not seem foreign in professional conversations.

People have a wide range of work options today, whether it be flextime, telecommuting, or various configurations of part-time, contingent, and contract work. This provides greater flexibility in shaping a work schedule in sync with our personal values and familial responsibilities.

Today we are seeing the beginnings of what I like to call *life-friendly* organizations. These organizations provide people with greater flexibility in balancing their work and personal lives. Daycare, whether on-site or subsidized by the employer off-site, and eldercare programs are increasingly common. They may soon become fixtures of the new work landscape.

Life-friendly organizations will value all contributors, whether they be full-time, contingent, or part-time 20-somethings or 50-somethings. They will be sensitive to the *entire* human life-cycle, reflecting the fact that people at different ages and career stages have varying needs, interests, commitments, and responsibilities. They will also recognize that people who *don't* have child care or eldercare responsibilities may still have personal needs and passions and commitments that need to be addressed.

At work, physical space will be organized to accommodate people working late at night, with TVs and couches for people who want to lie down and take a quick break. And instead of the traditional authoritarian structures of fixed spaces, spaces will become more fluid and flexible, with tactile, soft furniture. Traditional office chairs will be replaced with moveable futons. Recognizing the turbo-charged, over-committed lives of their employees, organizations will provide concierge-type services to help them, whether it be to pick up dry-cleaning, go to the shoemaker, or make special provisions for elderly parents.

You also have more flexibility in terms of how long you may choose to stay in a particular organization. In the days of fixed-benefit pension plans, people often felt compelled to continue in jobs they had come to detest. It was too expensive for them to move elsewhere and give up their accumulated future benefits (or "golden handcuffs"). Now, with portable pensions designed to reflect a more mobile and fluid economy, people are freer to move on without as much concern about the long-term financial consequences.

Freedom to Change: Role Fluidity

Elsewhere I have described the new workplace as "TempWorld," an arena where nothing is fixed or certain. In TempWorld, what we do to earn a living will constantly shift, from the content of our work to where we work and how we work. The result is more uncertainty – but also more *freedom* to take on new roles. Instead of being tied to fulfilling a particular role, or being stereotyped in that role throughout an entire career, we are now freer to sample different kinds of work and experience ourselves in different roles, whether as full-time employees, independent contractors, small-business owners, or professional temps.

This new fluidity of roles offers the prospect of tremendous liberation for those who dread being trapped in a particular role and who can't bear the thought that "I'm going to be doing the same thing for the rest of my life." Playing out different roles means we can develop a different understanding of ourselves in relation to our work environment and become freer to test out different aspects of our personality.

New career patterns reflect this shift from the old straight-line career. Instead of a predictable stride up a linear ladder, people will zigzag between different kinds of work situations, continually redeploying themselves in new ways as their work changes. Instead of, for example, being a corporate lawyer working your way up to partnership in the firm, you may be a recruiter specializing in hiring legal professionals, a legal textbook writer, or a corporate treasurer.

In fact, people today are increasingly playing multiple work roles. For example, combining teaching an evening course at university with consulting to startup companies and a regular two-day-a-week gig as a marketing manager. In this way, we can do a variety of stimulating work that reflects and plays to different aspects of our diverse interests and strengths.

Redefining Failure

In a work world of greater fluidity and mobility, the ability to take risks — to try on new roles, new challenges, and new ways of working — is a key determining factor in career success. But if risk-taking is celebrated, then we also need to adjust our reactions to the potential flipside of risk.

When people take risks, they sometimes fail. Indeed, when we look at the track record of successful entrepreneurs in starting new businesses, we see that many failed repeatedly before they finally got it right. Career activists, like entrepreneurs, must accept the potential to fail, and must learn to see failure in a different light.

In today's highly mobile economy, people lose jobs for a variety of reasons, most of them due to *change*. Personnel changes, for example, may lead to personality clashes; changing job requirements, to a bad person-job fit. Moreover, the more often we move around, the greater the probability of running into an untenable work situation. We need to learn to think of job loss in a new light, as simply being part of a new work landscape, something that happens as we move in and out of different income producing domains.

Indeed, people's attitudes to failure are already shifting. We are so information-overloaded and time-committed these days, and so prone to move around from one work situation to another, that our memories of our own and other people's failures has grown much shorter. Losing a job used to be an anguishing experience filled with a sense of failure. A friend's father-in-law, for example, still remembers being fired from his first job more than 40 years ago, and still wonders why. These days, few people who lose a job pause to look back. They simply get on with their lives.

Indeed, the time may come when we take a dim view of those who have never experienced any kind of failure. We may suspect them of not being sufficiently engaged by their world to take a calculated risk. People who have never failed may appear to us as overly rigid and programmed, unwilling to take an activist stance towards their career, always making "safe" choices.

Opportunity to Test Yourself

Increasingly, individuals who work for organizations are being empowered to make many more decisions regarding how they do their work and how they please customers. Organizations have become much flatter, with bureaucratic top-down decision-making being replaced by decision-making much closer to the front lines. At the same time, the sheer *speed* with which decisions must be made in today's volatile marketplace means there is no time for endless group decision-making, review, and discussion until consensus is achieved.

As decision-making gets pushed further and further down the line, people have more of an opportunity to test their individual effectiveness and judgment. One 40-year-old marketing professional, part of the senior-management group that had bought out his previous employer, told me, "It's the same products, and the same kind of decisions have to be made. But whereas before I would come to my team with pages of figures and pros and cons associated with making investments, I now have to make that decision myself without the benefit of group input or even the luxury of time. What's exciting is knowing you were the key person instrumental in the decision, and you're responsible for what happens."

Think of some of the words I have used to define some of the characteristics of the new workplace: zigzag between jobs and work domains, testing yourself, uncertainty. These words all suggest movement and change.

In the old-style career, you typically knew exactly where you were heading, whether you wanted to get there or not. The new career is much less predictable, and much more exciting. You can take steps to design your future, but you can never quite know where things will go. To use that trite expression, it's a journey of discovery, and in the true sense. If you have the fortitude, confidence in your skills, and emotional resilience to embrace it, it can be an exhilarating trip.

Redefining Time

When I was 22, having just graduated from McGill University, I went to Europe to travel. My parents told all their friends that I was "taking a year off." I was puzzled by their description of my behavior, as it seemed to imply that I had somehow ceased to exist in a meaningful way — as if the only way of being engaged in the world was either as a student or a worker.

In the new career, increasingly, we won't talk about time "on" and "off." All time will count, whether or not the way it was spent was instrumental in producing an income. This will be liberating in terms of the choices that people can make about how they spend their time after their earlier formal education.

Forty-nine-year-old Jocelyn B., for example, is at a crossroads in her career, finding herself doing work that is increasingly unsatisfying and unchallenging. She has decided to take a sabbatical to backpack in Asia. "Look at me," she says. "Isn't this extraordinary? Who would have thought a 49-year-old conservative executive would have aggressively lobbied to take a sabbatical with no particular plans as to whether I will return to my job?"

It used to be that the starting line was the first job, post-college or university. One then moved in a relatively predictable way through a series of linearly-structured career opportunities. Today, movement is much more fluid as we shuttle between different life spheres, be it work, education, leisure, or family commitments. And if there is no starting line or finishing line, then one is free to try out various kinds of career and life challenges.

In this scenario, all activity is legitimate. A career becomes a rich pattern of work and life experiences orchestrated by the individual spanning a broad range of potential experiences. That pattern will include work, study, travel, family, and time spent pursuing personal passions.

When you have belief in your own competence, you don't need to worry about taking time "off" or about an uncertain future. Instead, you can allow your career and your life to unfold through different spheres of experience, whether traveling the world, enhancing your education, or raising a family.

We will also see much greater acceptance of the possibility of successful *mid-career change* – something that in the past was often seen as misguided and bound to fail. For example, the legendary French writer Colette, approaching 60, decided to open a beauty salon in 1932. It was a bad time for the arts, and the effects of the Depression were beginning to be felt in France, so she needed a practical way to earn a living. Unfortunately, Parisians reacted negatively and scornfully. "My crime is serious," she wrote in French *Vogue*. "Starting a whole new career at an age when women are supposed to be over the hill."

In the past, when someone made a change in mid-career it was considered a huge deviation from the norm. Today, there is widespread recognition that we can and will reconfigure ourselves in different ways throughout our careers.

There is also no finishing line. Retirement is no longer the end of working life. The erosion of social programs, and doubts about the viability of government pension plans, mean that many people will need to continue to earn a living past 65. At the same time, we are living longer and healthier lives and need to remain intellectually and emotionally engaged, so that continuing to work meets our psychological needs as well.

So if you don't like what you are doing now, it's never too late to change things. You might find something else that is more to your liking – or someone might invent a job tomorrow that will fit you better.

Redefining Success

Darryl K., 48, was formerly the vice-president of marketing for a large petrochemical organization. When he was fired, he pounded the street. But like so many of his cohorts, he was not successful. But as a child, Darryl had always had a passion to act. "All of a sudden," he says, "I had an idea, which 10 years ago would have been unthinkable. I wanted to act. I told my wife, and thought she would think I was crazy. But instead, she said, 'Go for it.'" Darryl has taken a huge decrease in income, but for the first six months has managed to earn about $20,000 as a film extra and doing the occasional commercial.

Increasingly, the way in which we evaluate work is being liberated from pure considerations of money to a focus on the actual content of our work: what we like doing, what we do best, what is personally meaningful.

It's true, of course, that people always cared about the nature of their work and whether it was challenging. But they were also motivated by such external considerations as prestige, financial security, and status. Today the importance of these external considerations has been reduced, at least in relative terms, and internal rewards, such as personal fulfillment, have come to the forefront.

In part this is because for many people these external rewards are no longer so readily available: their prospects for further advancement are slim, or like Darryl they are having difficulty finding any kind of work. This forces them to look inward for their sense of career satisfaction. At the same time, the search for greater personal authenticity leads people to place greater value on the intrinsic qualities of work – in some cases rejecting prestige and money in favor of personal satisfaction and growth.

In the new career, rather than viewing career success purely in terms of status and monetary considerations, we will use other measures. When we look at our work, we will ask: Will I be free to pursue a passion? Will I learn? Will I be engaged? When redefined in this way, career success is within everyone's reach.

Opportunities for Authenticity

Laura F. was a 30-something successful lawyer with rosy prospects for becoming a partner in her high-profile firm. As a result of a messy divorce, she became increasingly worried about the effects of her 60-hour work week on her children. This in turn made her concerned about the psychological well-being of children in general. After doing some serious soul-searching, she took a significant decrease in income to start up a nonprofit agency devoted to promoting the wellness of children.

Today, people are demanding that their work reflect what they care about emotionally and intellectually. There has always been a tendency for people in mid-career to reevaluate whether they are doing work that is personally meaningful. Now, this is becoming a critical issue for everyone, including job entrants just out of school.

Being authentic means no longer pretending you are somebody else when you come to work. It means bringing your whole personality to work and doing work that is expressive of who you are in all aspects. Witness the many startups in high tech that have taken this to heart: the design of their offices, style of clothing, visual representation of the physical space reflect who the staff are and the nature of the work they are doing.

People in business are now much more open and self-expressive rather than impression-managing. They will tell people more personal things – that they don't like their job, for example, or that they are feeling stuck – where in the past they would have worried about saying something that might reflect badly on them. I've noticed, too, that people are more open in their business dealings. They used to be cagey when it came to talking about things like their budget for a particular project. Today, people are much more honest in expressing where they stand and what they are thinking and feeling. After all, who has time to play games?

Opportunity to Make Big Money

One can barely pick up a newspaper or magazine these days without reading about 20- or 30-somethings who parlayed their understanding of technology or popular culture, or their skills in some high-level scientific endeavor, into a fortune.

In an era where what you know, your ability to read the environment, extreme focus, and capacity to take risks count more than experience, anyone can potentially become the next Bill Gates at any age. And if you can't become the next Bill Gates, perhaps you can work for him or her – and get rich with them. Startup companies in high-growth areas such as high technology often offer stock options instead of a higher salary. In this way they can attract talented people with the promise of future wealth when the stock is publicly traded or the company is acquired. Sometimes these stock options prove to be very valuable – as witness the number of millionaires who work for Microsoft.

Even in more conventional organizations, an increasingly common feature of today's compensation schemes is having money at risk. Betting on the quality of your work can lead to significant rewards, whether it be in bonus, commission, or stock options.

Talent Pushes Back

As hyper-frenetic work schedules become the norm, people will increasingly demand of their employer that their hard work be recognized and rewarded with time off. People will refuse to be the servant of productivity-obsessed organizations. They will look at work and free time as coins to be bartered. They will say in essence, "I rose to the challenge of doing the work that needed to be done, but in exchange for these past eight days of round-the-clock work, I expect you to honor my time by giving me time off." In other words, hard work buys time for play.

Being an activist means that individuals will be prepared to *protest* about work expectations they perceive to be unreasonable. Freed up from a psychological mind-set that enforces dependence, they will see themselves as worthy of having all their work sacrifice honored. They will expect time in exchange for time, not a modest token such as "you can leave work early today."

Start Spreading the News

Heather was offered what she thought was the job of her dreams: she was going to be given complete autonomy to create and manage a new function that would develop a new marketing strategy. Unfortunately, the billing of the job far exceeded the reality. She had numerous conversations with her boss, but when he said, "There's going to be some changes around here, just hold on a bit longer and I promise you it will be worth your while," she quit.

"Life is too short," she said, "and work is too important to be living with this frustration. I deserve better than this. I'm out of here."

When you believe in your personal competence, are aware of your skill portfolio, and understand the new work landscape, you will have the confidence not only to expect but also to *demand* that your work meets your personal needs.

Conclusion

Work plays a crucial role in determining how we feel about ourselves: our self-esteem, our mental well-being, our ability to experience the world with joy and optimism, how we parent our children, and how we contribute to our individual workplaces, our communities, and our society. Given such significance, having work that engages us, makes us feel good about ourselves and allows us to play all the critical roles in our lives – partner, parent, friend, child, individual contributor, as well as citizen – is not a luxury, but a necessity.

It would be Pollyanna-ish of me not to acknowledge that there is a dark side to the new work landscape. But if we cultivate resilience, pluckiness, and a belief in the future, we can shape a work world that we will be proud to leave for the next generation.

Bon voyage!

About
Barbara Moses
"Canadian career guru" (Fast Company, October 1998)

Dr. Barbara Moses, North America's leading expert in career self-management, is the best-selling author of *Career Intelligence* and is the work issues columnist for Canada's national newspaper, the *Globe and Mail*.

Dr. Moses is also the author of the acclaimed *Career Planning Workbook* and *Manager's Career Coaching Guide*. Since its first publication in 1982, the *Career Planning Workbook* has become a "corporate bestseller," completed by over a million people in more than 2,000 organizations worldwide.

A sought-after presenter and keynote speaker for senior business and professional audiences, Dr. Moses is consistently praised for her practical insights into new work and personal realities, her stimulating and compelling delivery, and her tell-it-like-it-is style.

Dr. Moses' innovative approach to career self-management has been reported on extensively in numerous publications across North America. She has appeared frequently on network and local TV and radio and has been quoted and profiled in major North American publications, including *Fast Company* magazine, the *New York Times, Los Angeles Times, EnRoute, Parenting, Toronto Star*, the *Globe and Mail*, and *Report on Business Magazine*.

Dr. Moses holds degrees in psychology from McGill University, the London School of Economics, and the University of Toronto.

Clients

More than 2,000 organizations worldwide in every sector of the economy, including education, financial services, government, health care, high technology, mass media, oil and petrochemical, public accounting, telecommunications, and travel and hospitality.

Career Management Programs from
BBM Human Resource Consultants

The most pressing issues facing individuals and organizations today are self-management, managing change, employability, and learning for the future. Dr. Moses' firm, BBM Human Resource Consultants, provides proven interventions to prepare staff at all levels to meet these challenges and thrive in the new knowledge economy.

BBM shows organizations and individuals buffeted by change how to respond to the new career and work realities – promoting self-reliance and adaptation to change, managing work and personal life, motivating different demographic groups, advancing continuous learning, mentoring, and fostering renewal and revitalization. Over the past decade, BBM has helped thousands of organizations deliver career development and career self-management programs. A full-service firm, BBM provides career planning materials, workshops, and consulting support.

With its head office in Toronto, BBM has representative offices in Montreal; Calgary; Ottawa; Vancouver; New York; Chicago; Auckland, New Zealand; and London, UK.

Career Planning Workbook

A corporate best-seller, the *Career Planning Workbook* has helped over a million people worldwide manage their careers in the light of the new work and personal realities. It is a highly user-friendly, innovative, and cost-effective approach to providing comprehensive and practical career planning guidance.

Completing the *Career Planning Workbook* is like having your own personal career coach and counselor. Through a series of easy-to-complete self-assessment instruments, people identify core strengths and competencies; their unique profile of personal work style and preferences; and how to better balance competing demands of work and personal life, among other issues.

A highly flexible tool, the *Workbook* can be used on a self-study basis or in workshops, and is available in two editions – managerial/professional and clerical/technical – to provide professional quality career planning support to all staff.

Manager's Career Coaching Guide

This companion piece to the *Career Planning Workbook* prepares managers for their crucial role in developing and counseling staff; providing information and how-to advice on the new employment contract at work; dealing with coaching concerns; supporting career self-management; helping people cope with new work realities; and handling common career issues including burnout, plateauing, and Managing Generation X.

Workshops

A range of workshops are offered for different employee groups, including:
- Executive Overview
- Personal Career Self-Management Workshops
- Manager's Career Planning and Coaching Workshop
- Train-the-Trainer to Implement Career Self-Management

Keynote Speeches / Events by Dr. Barbara Moses

Extraordinary changes in the workplace have transformed the fundamental relationship between the individual and the organization. How do we have a sense of career, when everything we have been socialized to believe to be true is no longer true? In her lucid, compelling speeches, Dr. Moses provides insight into the new work and personal realities, along with practical strategies for dealing with them, and shows you how to profit from the good news about careers. Speeches are tailored to meet the needs and interests of different audiences, including women, managers, individual contributors, early-career professionals, and so on.

For more information on services from BBM Human Resource Consultants visit our web site at: http://www.BBMcareerdev.com